STARGAZER

PREDICTIONS & PROPHECIES

"The Man Who Predicted 9/11!"

Presenting…

ANTHONY CARR

"The World's *Most Documented* Psychic!"

White Knight Book Distribution Services Ltd

PUBLISHER'S NOTE

These predictions and prophesies were written and completed by June 30, 2006.

These include the world's first full face transplant; **CONRAD BLACK**'s U.S. indictment for fraud; "Kiss of death if Black retains Greenspan;" (to wit: "Black fires Greenspan, after losing trial," *Toronto Star*); **SYLVESTER STALLONE** making yet another Rocky and Rambo movie; **BARBRA STREISAND** abandoning retirement to tour once more; the completely unexpected earthquake that shook Barrie, Ontario, Canada (virtually an earthquake-free zone!); * **SIMPSON** once more being thrust into the spotlight (temporarily) where he "somehow confesses." (To wit: "**O.J.** has just signed a 5 million dollar U.S. book deal for 'his version' of the case"); Korea detonating a nuclear weapon, to the consternation of the world; WWII veteran Pima Native American **IRA HAYES**, who helped raise the flag over IWO JIMA, will be honored in one way or another; to wit: **CLINT EASTWOOD**'s *Flags Of Our Fathers* and the death of U.S. President **GEORGE W. BUSH!** (At least at the movies: *Death of A President —* namely, **GEORGE W. BUSH!**), *Apocalypto* (see page 12), and "Dead legs walk again!" (see *PageTen*, *Toronto Sun*, December 3, 2006: "Cheryl Paget, as a result of stem cell research in China, now can move her legs! Very encouraging for someone with a broken back!").

I hope you enjoy this book, and thank you for purchasing it.

ISBN 978-1897456026

Carr, Anthony
STARGAZER
Predictions and Prophesies

Published by
White Knight Book Distribution Services Ltd
Suite 304, 160 Balmoral Avenue
Toronto, Ontario, Canada M4V 1J7

Printed and Bound in Canada

This Book is Dedicated to *Me*,
without whose persistence,
determination and genius the
following pages would not
be possible...

Anthony Carr

ACKNOWLEDGEMENTS

My thanks go out to the following people for their excellent contributions to my book, and to my life.

Allen Spraggett Doctor of Divinity, former religion editor of the *Toronto Star* and author of fourteen books on the paranormal. A genius whose knowledge is truly encyclopedic, he is a living, walking university who has passed on much of his erudition to me (at any rate, as much as I can absorb) and possesses the patience of Job in forever buffeting the tidal wave of my Sisyphean questions about "the meaning of life." (He is also responsible for my very first television appearance.) For all of this, I am deeply grateful to him.

Les Pyette (Emeritus CEO, *Toronto Sun* Publishing Corporation and *National Post*), without whose "nose for news" and special "insight" most of my projects never would have seen the light of day. This puts him head and shoulders above the sea of journalists, for which I shall always be indebted.

To the memories of CFRB's legendary **Gordon Sinclair** (author of *The Americans*), late *Toronto Sun* columnists **Paul "The Rimmer" Rimstead, George Cunningham-Tee** and dear **Dave Bailey** for their encouragement, support and mentorship; and to **Glen Woodcock** (who is still on the earth plane), for opening the door.

The talented **Ray Parrish** for his wonderful illustrations and editorial input.

Carola Vyhnak (*Toronto Star*) for having the guts to publish many of my outrageous and startling predictions beforehand — namely 9/11! **B.J. DelConte** (former UPI Bureau Chief and CITY-TV talk show host), for his support.

Richard McIlveen (CFTO-TV News Producer), for providing me an annual platform from which to broadcast my New Year predictions, in spite of heavy opposition from his "higher ups."

Former *National Enquirer, Examiner* and *Globe* editor **Joe Mullins** for introducing my work to the highly entertaining and often controversial world of the tabloids, lo these many years ago.

Ben E. King (of "Stand By Me" fame), for generously donating his valuable time and name to my projects and world predictions.

Kenise and the late **Fintan Kilbride**, respectively of Ryerson University (professor of early childhood education) and Neil McNeill High School (English and Latin), for their bulwark toleration of my interminable questions about grammar and prose. Bless you both.

Legendary **"Rompin´ " Ronnie Hawkins**, who gave me my first job (as a saxophone player) and has guided me though my career with his colorful, cracker-barrel philosophies.

Tina and Paul Higgins, psychics both, for their priceless annual evaluation of my long list of predictions, without whose common sense advice I would be making a bigger fool of myself than I already am.

Justin Da Silva, cover and interior design, technical editor.

2001 'will put fear of God in us,' psychic says

Anthony Carr foresees 'cataclysmic cosmic event' shocking world

BY CAROLA VYHNAK
TORONTO STAR

LOOK UP, way up. Toronto psychic Anthony Carr feels it, senses it coming.

It is an imminent "cataclysmic cosmic event," advises Carr, who has been making a living telling people about his premonitions for 35 years.

"Watch for a sign in the heavens. It will shock the whole world. It could be like a bolt of lightning or in the form of a UFO — a mighty astronaut."

The event "will put the fear of God into us," predicts the east-end psychic and palmist who counts Hollywood stars among his clients.

"What I feel for the world is a great revelation, as if the entire population is coming to its collective senses. It's as though we realize we have to do something before it's too late."

That something, he continues, means we should "re-green the planet, unpollute the waters, feed the starving."

The revelation will herald a return to old-fashioned values in which more people marry and stay together, Carr predicts.

"The 'me' syndrome will be gone. We'll help each other and band together for protection and for the sake of survival of the human race."

Carr claims his share of success with his visions and premonitions. He predicted the death of Princess Diana, accusations of corruption and racketeering against former prime minister Brian Mulroney and also Bloc Québécois leader Lucien Bouchard's battle with flesh-eating disease.

In his own words: "Anthony Carr is so chillingly accurate that he has been hailed by reputable media persons as a modern-day Nostradamus."

The clairvoyant, who calls himself "the world's most documented psychic," has been in newspapers, tabloids and on radio and television programs.

"I go through all the newspapers, listen to the radio, watch movies. If a certain thing catches me, twigs me, I go with it."

He foresees events and experiences through a feeling, a vision or telepathy in which he picks up something from an individual "on the other side of the world."

He picked up vibes from Scotland where Madonna married British filmmaker Guy Ritchie in an extravagant wedding on Dec. 22.

"This marriage is doomed," says Carr, who previously predicted motherhood (two children) for the superstar singer. "They're a Virgo and a Leo

ANTHONY CARR: "Watch for a sign in the heavens. It will shock the whole world," says prominent Toronto psychic who also predicts the Leafs will win the Stanley Cup in 2001.

VINCE TALOTTA/TORONTO STAR

— forget it. I give them a couple of years. He'll want to rule the roost and she won't let him."

A few years ago, after coming out of a movie starring Arnold Schwarzenegger, Carr saw a large, cut-out figure of the actor in the lobby. Arnie's arm was reaching up with his hand spread out and Carr was able to read his palm.

"All of a sudden," he recalls, "I got a sharp feeling in my chest, just like a wave came through here. I thought: 'This guy's gonna have a serious heart attack.'"

When he warned Schwarzenegger,

Carr says, the actor was stunned.

"He had a huge hole in his aortic valve — a congenital heart defect — and no one knew he had it but him."

Schwarzenegger subsequently underwent elective surgery in 1997 to repair the valve.

Carr includes Canadian movie megastar Jim Carrey on his list of predictions for 2001, saying the rubber-faced comic will make "lavish contributions" to homeless shelters and the poor in Toronto.

"He was a Cabbagetown kid," Carr notes. "He doesn't forget where he came from."

Carrey is "eternally paranoid" about losing his fame and fortune, Carr says, and the Hollywood star feels compelled to share his wealth, lest he become "overwhelmed by guilt over his success."

So much for the good news. Carr is also picking up bad vibes from the heavens. He predicts a "great economic crash" early in the year, as the euro becomes worthless and the Canadian dollar slips downward.

His advice is to stay calm and play it safe. "Don't spend any money, don't invest — keep it in the bank. Don't panic."

If you have stocks, he adds, don't start selling. "Not only does haste make waste but greed makes waste."

His advice on life and love? "Let your instincts be your guide. They will always tell you the way to go."

Other Carr predictions for 2001:

■ The Leafs will win the Stanley Cup.

■ The Argos will prevail in the Grey Cup and the Blue Jays will take the

☛ Please see Carr's, F2

Local boy makes good

We weren't surprised to read — on the Web and in usually reliable publications — a bogus prediction supposedly made by Nostradamus about the terrorist attacks on New York. We were still embarrassed that we bought an earlier phony prophecy attributed to the 16th-century soothsayer about the U.S. electing a "village idiot" as President.

Then we recalled a Star story about Toronto psychic Anthony Carr, which ran last New Year's Eve, in which he foresaw an imminent "cataclysmic cosmic event."

"Watch for a sign in the heavens. It will shock the whole world. It could be like a bolt of lightning or in the form of a UFO — a mighty astronaut" and would "put the fear of God into us," writer Carola Vyhnak quoted him as saying.

"What I feel for the world is a great revelation, as if the entire population is coming to its collective senses. It's as though we realize we have to do something before it's too late," Carr continued.

The revelation would herald a return to old-fashioned values in which more people marry and stay together, he added. "The 'me' syndrome will be gone. We'll help each other and band together for protection and for the sake of survival of the human race." Yikes.

Word of Mouse will return

THE TORONTO STAR

SPORTS *plus*

■ NFL
Big day for Rams, Steelers, Eagles

Monday, December 31, 2001

■ WORLD JUNIORS
Finland 4
Canada 1

thestar .com

The future

VINCE TALOTTA/TORONTO STAR FILE PHOTO

HEAVENLY GUIDANCE: Anthony Carr says he predicted the events of Sept. 11 with 100 per cent accuracy.

Challenging a psychic

Re *Medium is messenger*, Dec. 28.

Once again, The Star has published a story on the paranormal by referring to some East-end, so-called psychic's ability to predict future events as "accurate." If this were done in the spirit of, say, humour, I would not see a problem. But when the media intentionally misinforms the public, we must call it what it is: irresponsible. Do you really believe Anthony Carr has the ability to predict future events? If you do, why? To echo Socrates and the ancient Sceptics, is it not the responsibility of every person to seriously reflect on their beliefs and to question why it is they believe what they

do? Was it not a lack of reflection that brought about the Sept. 11 tragedies? Beliefs do influence actions (does Carr make any money from his psychic abilities?). If you believe that Carr's predictions come from a genuine capacity to see the future, then we have an obligation to examine this wonderful gift more carefully.

So consider this an open invitation for Carr and The Star to visit the University of Guelph, where I teach critical thinking. Together, with the aid of the Committee for the Scientific Investigation of Claims of the Paranormal, we shall examine Carr's past track record and con-

sider his predictions for 2002.

And of course, The Star's journalists will do the responsible thing and print the results of our meeting while keeping tabs on Carr's predictions for 2002. This will definitely validate Carr's wonderful gift and establish him as the genuine psychic The Star claims him to be.

As the winter semester is about to begin, I cannot think of a better way to introduce to my students a more interesting experiment in rational responsibility.

CHRISTOPHER DiCARLO
Department of Philosophy
University of Guelph
Guelph

TORONTO STAR

Psychic's prediction was close

Re *Where were the psychics?* Letter, Nov. 13.

Jacob Mendlovic asked why no psychic foresaw the events of Sept. 11. Anthony Carr was nearly bang on in his prediction in The Star article, 2001 *'will put fear of God in us,' psychic says,* Dec. 31. The article said: "Look up, way up. Toronto psychic Anthony Carr feels it, senses it coming. It is an imminent 'cataclysmic cosmic event,' advises Carr. 'Watch for a sign in the heavens. It will shock the whole world. It could be like a bolt of lightning or in the form of a UFO.'"

It was aircraft that came out of the heavens on Sept. 11 so Carr wasn't far off.

The article continued: "The event 'will put the fear of God into us,' predicts the east-end psychic. 'What I feel for the world is a great revelation … It's as though we realize we have to do something before it's too late.' That something, he continues, means we should 're-green the planet, unpollute the waters, feed the starving.'"

JEANETTE BLONSKI
Richmond Hill

EXPERTS REPORT: OLDER WOMEN MAKE BETTER WIVES — *& LOVERS!*

Woman's face **BLOWS UP** after hair dye horror!

Julia Roberts vs. Sandra Bullock
NASTY FEUD OVER BEN

NATIONAL Examiner
AMERICA'S FAVORITE FAMILY WEEKLY

January 16, 2001

$1.79 / $2.29 CANADA

HIS KIDS ARE NO-SHOWS AT FINAL FAREWELL!

NEW REAGAN TRAGEDY

MARIE OSMOND
How she saved her marriage

WIN CASH!
4 DIFFERENT PUZZLES

Pal Vinnie Jones (left) with wife Tanya and Guy Ritchie with Madonna

Madonna's hoppin' mad at Travolta

MADONNA wants revenge on John Travolta for ruining her wedding.

Travolta, 46, forbade soccer star-turned-actor Vinnie Jones, 35, from being best man for the singer's movie director groom, Guy Ritchie, 32, so Jones could finish making a movie Travolta is directing in America.

John Travolta

Jones expects to earn $2.25 million for his role in Swordfish, for which Travolta is also a co-star. But when Jones asked for time off to stand up for Ritchie, Travolta reportedly railed: "You can't go. We've got a movie to make."

John refused Guy's pal Vinnie time off to go to the wedding

With 48 hours' warning, Ritchie had to find another pal to fill the role in the star-studded wedding at Skibo Castle in Scotland. And neither Madonna nor Ritchie could get Travolta on the phone to negotiate on the nuptials.

Jones ended up sending a video of himself toasting the couple, which was played on a giant monitor during the service.

Not good enough, says The Material Bride.

"John Travolta's ruined my wedding," Madonna told a pal. "And I'll never forgive him.

"But I'll get him back. And I hope he remembers these words — payback's a bitch."

2001 PREDICTIONS

ROYAL scandal. A woman president or vice president. Political and economic upheaval. Miraculous cures and murderous disease. Death by natural disaster and terrorism.

All this and more has been revealed to a foremost psychic while peering into the future for National EXAMINER readers. Here are the predictions from world-famous prognosticator Anthony Carr for 2001 and beyond:

■ Hillary Clinton will become the first U.S. woman vice president or president by 2008.

■ Prince Charles will publicly turn his back on the British royal throne for emotional reasons, opening the way for someone else, but not Princes William or Harry — possibly Andrew!

■ Former Yugoslovian dictator Slobodan Milosevic will attempt a vicious military coup, but to no avail. He'll eventually be executed for

■ Former Spin City star Michael J. Fox will be completely cured of Parkinson's disease even before two years have passed.

crimes against humanity.

■ The Empire State Building explodes from a terrorist bomb! Arab terrorists — who wear the red turban and whose emblem is "a star and crescent moon" — are responsible for this futile attempt to demoralize America.

■ An earthquake and a tidal wave hit Boston, Mass., of all places.

■ The tag-team of Gorby and Boris will initiate a world power play in 2001. Russia, beware of Mikhail Gorbachev and Boris Yeltsin.

■ Bulgaria explodes! I see crushing khaki tanks on whose sides are emblazoned a great red star.

■ A horrific Spanish flu-like virus will sweep around the world, destroying more human life than did the previous two World Wars. It will originate in India. I believe Spanish flu-infected human tissue still preserved from the early 1900s will be the culprit.

■ Residents around The Three Mile Island nuclear plant in Pennsylvania will hold their collective breath while news of another leak goes public. The narrow escape will force new safety regulations for nuclear power plants across America and, I might add, Canada. Toronto, take note!

■ Tina Sinatra, in her new book My Father's Daughter, insults Frank's widow Barbara. They come to blows in a clash on Larry

NATIONAL EXAMINER (ISSN 1094-0655) Published weekly by National Examiner, Inc., Boca Raton, FL 33487. Vol. 38 — No. 03. Editorial offices 5401 N.W. Broken Sound Blvd., additional offices. Periodical registration number 1563. Postmaster: Send address changes to National EXAMINER, P.O. Box 420235, Palm Coast, FL 32142-0235. For subscription

BALD GORBY – BEAUTY OR THE BEAST

Anthony Carr, noted psychic, confronted Gorbachev recently In Toronto at a Variety Village tour. Carr believes the mark on Gorby's Forehead indicates he could be "The Beast" referred to in Revelations 13.

"...One of its heads '*seemed*' to have a mortal wound, but its mortal wound was healed..."

Bald Gorby - Beauty or The Beast

Anthony Carr noted psychic-palmist confronted Gorbachev
recently in Toronto at a Variety Village tour. Carr believes the
mark on Gorby's forehead indicates he could be "The Beast"
referred to in Revelations 13.

CFTO-TV

*"...One of its heads 'seemed' to have a
mortal wound, but its wound was healed,..."*
(REV. 13:3)

Get ready for Canada's Premier Psychic Anthony Carr!!! His soon to
be released <u>Specific Predictions</u> are uncannily accurate when
predicting world matters. "Especially relating to the medical field",
notes Shirley of <u>The Shirley Show</u>. Carr is the accurate psychic
palmist or Chiropsychologist that his long list of celebrity
endorsements attest to; **Mikhail Gorbachev** was the last famous
recipient of Carr's predictions. It was April 7th that Toronto's CFTO-TV
covered Carr confronting **Gorby** with the prediction that he will return
to the world stage with a position of immense power. Also, the mark
on **Mr. Gorbachev's** forehead indicated to Carr that he could be "The
Beast" referred to in the Book of Revelations. The man, Carr, is no
stranger to controversy. Even on his last visit to New York City he
remarked at how amazed he was that there was no trouble with his
visit. Who would have guessed that **Michael Jackson's** career would
hit the skids due to a bizarre, sex-related scandal, but Carr saw this
in his mind's eye and had published it in his <u>Specific Predictions</u>.

- more -

Medium is messenger

Toronto psychic who foretold 9/11 events predicts bin Laden's surrender

By CAROLA VYHNAK
TORONTO STAR

The Sept. 11 terrorist attacks should have come as no surprise to Anthony Carr. After all, the psychic predicted the events with — in his words — "dead-on, 100 per cent accuracy."

The psychic part of him had "seen" it coming when he did his predictions for 2001 in October 2000 and again last August.

"I see a terrible plane crash over New York City," he wrote. "I see raging fires around the White House in Washington, D.C. A great disaster will strike a major city to create a yawning chasm as earth and buildings topple into eternity."

Looking at the bigger picture, the east-end psychic and palmist also foresaw a "cataclysmic cosmic event" that would shock the world and "put the fear of God in us."

Carr derives no satisfaction from being right. "Despite my bravado and glib attitude, they (accurate predictions) shock and frighten me half to death."

His ability to see the future, he explains, comes from his "third eye.

"I put myself in an altered state of consciousness — which is really an electrical state — so the cosmos will bombard my antennae."

Carr then becomes the messenger, taking the images and translating them into words. Those words add up to 30 pages of predictions for 2002, including the fate of Osama bin Laden.

In a "letter" to the terrorist leader, Carr says he "sees" his arms above his head in a posture of surrender. "Then you will suffer a most ignoble death at the hands of those you persecuted." The "very fatal and final denouement" will occur in mid-February, he says.

More locally, Toronto will be hit by a sizeable earthquake, Carr predicts, and a new provincial leader to replace outgoing Premier Mike Harris will bring back "real common sense" and return Ontario to an "even keel" in the areas of health, education and help for the homeless.

Prime Minister Jean Chrétien is heading for a shocking scandal involving a wealthy, eccentric woman. The strain of the ensuing media frenzy over the affair will cause him to step down from office. "A real cause célèbre, it'll be both noble and scandalous, for love or money — or both," says Carr. Chrétien's replacement, he adds, will be a woman "of extraordinary kindness."

On the sports front, the Leafs will win the Stanley Cup in 2002 (oops, Carr predicted that for 2001), but Blue Jays fans will have to wait to 2008 for a World Series victory.

Carr, who counts Hollywood personalities among his clients, devotes 15 pages of predictions to the entertainment scene. Singer Celine Dion, he says, will become so paranoid about flying that she'll buy and equip her own luxurious train car to travel with her "ailing husband" and young child.

Harry Potter creator J.K. Rowling will be accused of plagiarism by a "green-eyed woman" and will have to defend herself in court. She'll be vindicated but lacks the wizardry to remove the tarnish from her reputation. So says Anthony Carr — without the aid of a crystal ball.

FUTURE TENSE: According to Anthony Carr, Prime Minister Chrétien will leave office due to a scandal involving a woman, Celine Dion will be riding the rails with her "ailing husband" René Angelil and baby; Charles, and Osama bin Laden's days are numbered at about 45.

See pages 2,3,4,5&6

"THE WORLD'S <u>MOST</u> DOCUMENTED PSYCHIC"

ANTHONY CARR'S PREDICTIONS FOR ☞2001☜ -- AND BEYOND!!

WORLD EVENTS

Istanbul, once Constantinople, will be devastated by an unimaginably powerful earthquake early in the New Year, as will Los Angeles, New York and Toronto (much less so).

Terrible plane crash over **Toronto**. Hundreds killed!

Volcanoes world-wide will erupt en-masse with such force as to destroy old ones and create new ones. Watch out for Mt. St. Helen!

Champion race car driver **Mario Andretti** to be involved in horrific vehicular fatality (red car)!

I do believe **Hillary Clinton** will become the first U.S. woman Vice-President or President by 2008.

Dr. Elizabeth Kubler-Ross will soon become one of the subjects of her own best-selling book: "The Five Steps of Death and Dying!"

With the new administration in the U.S. comes a new and improved medical plan for the nation, and especially the poor.

Prince Charles will "publicly" turn his back on the British Royal Throne, for emotional reasons, opening the way for someone else, not Prince William or Harry. Possibly Andrew!

TITANIC II, now under construction, will come to a terrible end! Do <u>not</u> tempt <u>F</u>ate!

The trial of three British Columbia men charged with the largest mass murder in Canadian history -- the 1985 bombing of an Air-India flight that killed 329 people --will set off demonstrations world-wide, both here and in India, causing that country to temporarily become a nuisance to all nations.

Jean Vanier, Theologian and founder of L'Arche (community homes around the world), although a beautiful man who does beautiful work, will have his peaceful persona rocked by scandal. It will be the toughest test of his life.

Former Yugoslavian dictator, **Slobodan Milosevic** will attempt a vicious military coup, but to no avail. He'll eventually be executed for crimes against humanity.

Harlingen, Texas, home of the famous Iwo Jima statue of U.S. Marines raising the American flag over that most costly South Pacific island (in terms of lives lost: 6,821 Marines and Naval personnel) will unfortunately be hit by a ferocious hurricane, then a tornado, while a coastal tidal wave the size of the Empire State Building sweeps across the nearest coastline.

Poppies will grow on the grave of WW II Iwo Jima veteran Ira Hayes, an Arizona Pima tribe native, as a symbol of the innocence of his soul.

➡️ **The Empire State Building explodes from a terrorist bomb! In a futile attempt to demoralize America, Arab terrorists, who wear the red turban and whose emblem is a "star and crescent moon," are responsible.** ✓

➡️ **Sabotage of the D.C. senate building (white dome) -- black smoke and fire!** ✓

Very severe earthquakes and fires in **Southern California** -- this coming summer.

Earthquake and tidal wave to hit **Boston, Mass**; of all places.

A fatal outbreak of "Mad Cow Disease" strikes Toronto, moves across Canada, then spreads quickly to the U.S. where it wreaks havoc in America.

The outrageous murder of **Brazil's** street kids will come to a halt when world pressure and a new hero following in the footsteps of the late saviour of children, **Yves de Roussan**, forces new protective legislation.

➡️ **The Mideast will explode like a roman candle in 2001, drawing all nations ever closer to WW III!** ✓

Warships and ICBM's in and around **Australia and New Zealand!**

Great **economic crash** coming! January-February of 2001, as the Euro-dollar becomes worthless, the Canadian "peso" even less, while American currency remains relatively stable; yet Toronto, Vancouver, Montreal and the rest of Canada will thrive in the film industry because of it; entertainment in general --

83.   A "cosmic" fireworks display will rain down over Toronto, Canada.

84.   **Niagara Falls** will make world headlines when a small plane crashes into the river and is swept away. Two are rescued.

85.   A lot of construction, activity, jobs and increased waterflow draw international attention.

86.   Over the next few years, India will beocme militarily powerful under the leadership of a "warrior-prince who wears a red turban". I also see the Taj Mahal.

87.   "London Bridge is falling down" -- an explosion.

88. ➡ I see raging fires around the White House in Washington, D.C. !! ✓

89.   The Eiffel Tower will be bombed, and eventually toppled.

90.   The situation in the Middle East will erupt into another "Gulf War", and calmed down by a powerful political figure for a while. Then there will be a final confrontation which will involve the whole world.

91.   Comedienne Phyllis Diller must guard her health closely. Her nervous system will be strained to the limit when she takes on a terrific new television project, giving her career a much-needed boost. Also, problems with her children will take their toll.

92.   Frank Sinatra will begin talking about his late mother, as a new awareness evolves; likewise, Perry Como.

Page 12 next...

ANTHONY CARR'S 101 PREDICTIONS FOR 1996 – AND BEYOND!

1. As I have predicted for years, Quebec is now "defacto" gone from Canada. Before the next federal election, Canada will have separated. Quebec is gone from the Canadian scene; by this time next year, they'll be even goner! Jacques Parizeau will "pay" dearly for his treasonous act. The former Quebec Premier faces grave health crisis; a great "light" above and around his head. Jacques Parizeau, like the former Quebec premieer Rene Levesque – and the very nearly late Bloc Quebecois Party Leader and soon-to-be Quebec Premier and former Federal Leader of the Opposition, Lucien Bouchard, will suffer a similar Fate – only worse! – simply becuase his dream to destroy Canada will succeed!

2. Upon Quebec's declaration of sovereignty, the United States will immediately step in to take a very firm "foothold". I see American dollars falling from the skies into Quebec.

3. As I predicted before, billions and billions of dollars will pour into Canada through casinos, movie making and the hospitality industry – creating thousand upon thousands of jobs. Canada will enjoy a three-year financial boom.

4. Americans will have a new and improved medical plan for everyone, a cross between Canadian socialized medicine and the current American insurance plan.

5. ➡ **A successful bombing of the Staten Island Ferry! New York City will be rocked by multiple disasters; riots, earthquakes, chemical spills, and successful bombing.** ✓

6. Stately homes will once again grace the Toronto Islands. There will be no connecting link form the mainland (i.e. tunnel or bridge).

7. Toronto Mayor, Barbara Hall, will wear her official Chain-Of-Office to greet an incredibly famous figure: U.S. President Bill Clinton!

8. Clinton pulls off the impossible! He's re-elected!

9. A tremendous explosion and fire beneath Toronto's Union Station – Esplanade District! A terrible underground explosion and fire beneath the Esplanade! (Methane gas?) Sudden earthquake will hit Toronto! Toronto, in spite of everything, will prosper financially, socially and culturally.

'The beams are coming directly at you, and the side of the boat is disappearing'

JOHN ROCA/KRT

Deadly aftermath Emergency vessels approach the ferry that slammed into a Staten Island pier yesterday, killing 10 people and injuring dozens.

10 die in New York ferry disaster

Vessel slams into Staten Island pier
Boat's pilot flees, shoots himself

JANNY SCOTT
NEW YORK TIMES

NEW YORK—A Staten Island ferry moving at a rapid clip in gusting winds crashed into a pier at the St. George ferry terminal yesterday afternoon, killing 10 people and injuring dozens of others.

The concrete and wood pier sliced through the boat's side, mowing down tourists and commuters.

The exact cause of the 3:20 p.m. accident was not clear last night. But law enforcement officials said the ferry's pilot fled the scene to his home, barricaded himself in a bathroom, slit his wrists and shot himself twice in the chest with a powerful pellet gun.

The pilot, identified by city officials as Richard Smith, survived and was in critical condition at a local hospital, where detectives were waiting to interview him.

Smith was in charge of the boat when it neared the Staten Island terminal at a high speed, and his captain noticed that the ferry was off course, according to one police official.

➤ Please see **Ferry, A21**

Passenger ferry crashed into dock; at least 10 killed

NEW YORK

Hudson R.

NEW JERSEY

Whitehall Ferry Terminal

Manhattan

Staten Island

Brooklyn

Lower New York Bay

5 km

AP GRAPHIC

Anthony Carr
Toronto, Ontario

Visit to Vancouver reveals psychic prediction by Anthony Carr, "The World's Most Documented Psychic"!

While on plane, psychic suddenly struck by vision of terrible plane crash over New York City – hundreds killed.

On August 14, 2001, Anthony Carr visited Vancouver to record his mid-year predictions. On the first of these 4 tapes, you hear Anthony's prediction of a fatal plane crash over New York City. His exact words:

"I see a terrible plane crash over New York City – hundreds are killed."

These predictions were recorded and witnessed by :

Dave Jepkcott
Empire Marketing Corp.

Angi Cividino

Sheryl Hanula

Deon-Scott

What People Are Saying About Anthony Carr:

Anthony has read for the crowned heads of Europe and Hollywood—including Sylvester Stallone, Richard Burton, Lillian Gish, Liv Ullman, Peggy Lee, James Doohan ("Beam me up, Scotty!"), Mikhail Gorbachev, Phyllis Diller, Queen Juliana (of the Netherlands), Lady Iris Mountbatten (cousin to Queen Elizabeth), Elke Sommer, Douglas Fairbanks, Jr., Kato Katlin (O.J.'s houseboy), "Shock Jock" Howard Stern, Roseanne Barr, Jon Stewart (*The Daily Show*) and Academy Award winner Glenda Jackson, now leader of Britain's Labor Party.

"His track record for predicting major events is well-documented and truly astounding." (Mark Bonokoski—editor, Ottawa Sun)

"Dubbed 'the seer without peer,' Anthony Carr is the internationally acclaimed psychic-to-the-stars who foresees with chilling accuracy the events that shake and shape our world, and has often been hailed by reputable media persons as a modern day Nostradamus!" (B.J. Del Conte—Toronto Bureau Chief of United Press International [UPI] News Agency)

From the late Tom Snyder with regard to one of Anthony's predictions about him on his LATE, LATE SHOW? "Mr. Carr ... from your mouth to God's ear."

"He is this country's most published and respected psychic and palmist ..." (Ted Woloshyn—CFRB Radio, Toronto).

"The more bizarre Anthony's predictions, the more accurately they are fulfilled! I find him quite remarkable...." (ENERGY - 108 (Radio) Breakfast Show with Anwar Knight).

"What is this—Anthony Carr's Psychic Line? What are you—a comedian and a Psychic?!" (Howard Stern).

"You're crazy! How could you know those things about me? Nobody else does!" (Roseanne Barr)

Anthony Carr's Predictions for the Coming Years

As I sit here, pen in hand, attempting to ponder the Imponderable, I have come to accept with calm certainty, as only a person weary of fighting against the inevitable can, that The Skein of Destiny which weaves its way through all our lives is as inescapable and unalterable as Life and Death itself. Our Fate and that of the World was written in The Sands of Time and in The Stars in Heaven long before we ever arrived and there is not one single thing that any of us can do to change it.

There seems to be prevalent these days a groundswell of uneasiness felt by the peoples of the world, especially "Baby Boomers," the generation born of my era, roughly between 1940 and 1949. A sense of impending doom, that something is coming down the pike! (And maybe they're right!) "I was born during a war and probably will die during a war!" —is the oft-repeated refrain heard these days around the world. This "ill-feeling" has been created by the transiting "bolt out of the blue planet" Uranus, which left the sign of Aquarius where it sat comfortably for seven years and produced a "feel good" period of excitement and adventure because it formed a favorable trine (a 120 degree angle) to the natal Uranus in Gemini, where it was in 1940 to 1949 when this generation was born.

(By-the-bye, transiting means the signs in which the planets are *now, today, moving through the Heavens*; and natal means whatever signs *those same planets were going through on the day you were born*— and then were instantly frozen in Space and Time—frozen the moment the Universe snapped a picture of it, a picture attached to you for the duration of this life's experience — *and possibly the next.*)

Unfortunately the transiting Uranus of today has moved out of Aquarius and into Pisces, thus creating a square or a 90 degree angle to the natal Uranus in Gemini, now causing all this personal uneasiness—not to mention all kinds of unexpected world chaos and upset! (Giant killer tsunamis, etc.) This occurs because the delicate Electrical balance of Life in each of us and in our Solar System and Universe (and Multi-verse), right down to the cellular level of the amoeba, has been upset (to say the least); so our general "feeling of uneasiness" is well-founded. But fear not, for this too shall soon pass.

Get ready for the new phenomenon of "Re-birth charts." You probably know your own birth sign, most people do. What you may not be so familiar with is who or what you were in a previous existence (if such a thing exists), that is to say, a previous existence of your Electrical Energy Field, whence your future incarnation may be determined!

When you "gasp your last," the exact moment "you shed this mortal coil," an astrologer can make a Re-birth chart based on the position of the planets in the heavens the instant you pass on, and then perhaps tell you who or what you will return as, the moment you exit then enter your new receptacle. If you return as human, you can will your estate to your future self. If as animal, then leave your goods to the ASPCA (American Society for the Prevention of Cruelty to Animals) or the Canadian Humane Society. And if mineral or vegetable, maybe donate to your favorite botanical or geological society. Yes! I predict Re-birth charts will soon be in vogue. (…Or maybe not.)

* * *

Coming World Events:

Flee! — Flee to the mountain tops! — the darkest caves! — the bowels of the earth!
World War III is upon us! The Mideast ignites like a Roman candle! This "*skirmish*" is aught but a prelude to global conflagration!!!
A never-ending chain reaction — this oscillating conflict between Muslim and Jew—will now draw in every nation on Earth! Increasing exponentially it is a pebble tossed onto the millpond of humanity, its stillness forever shattered, its ever widening circle engulfing all within range…. Nor shall the West escape:

"… Be not Smug, o ye on foreign shores; for I shall rain down fire and brimstone upon thy heads…." (Christian Bible)

Oh — horror of horrors! Only divine intervention — the "Lord of Host"— can cease the destruction! Whether God be Spirit or Star-traveler, perhaps from a distant galaxy beyond Space and Time, only from Him can Man hope to escape the complete carnage! ("... Lest all flesh perish!..." Christian Bible)

Science will soon prove that *precognition* (forecasting the future) has less to do with superstition and more to do with the natural laws of physics!

Just as a television *camera* converts images into electromagnetic frequencies and a television *set* converts those frequencies *back* into its *original* image, so too the individual life of every human being who ever walked or ever will walk this earth — indeed, even the entire planet itself with all its checkered and multi-layered past (Dinosaurs, Napoleon, Hitler, Caesar, etc) — will be recorded by that "Great Cosmic Camera in the Sky," to be filed away for All Time in the Universal Video Store, information to be retrieved at a later date. (Perhaps called The Book of Life?) Our dreams and "imaginings" are basically 3-D (three-dimensional) pictures captured and recorded both *within* and *without* simultaneously.

It is also the method by which psychics function: All dreams are merely visits to other Universes (or Universi). The images we carry *within* our mini-electrical computers, that is to say, our very own individual *physical electric brain* (the micro-"chip," as it were), is *only* the electrical component *which is separate* from the Universal Mind Which it (the mini-Mind *in* the brain) *serves;* that Electrical Mind, the individual Spark, Which is *not* the physical brain, in turn is *part and parcel* of the Great Electrical Mind Beyond — that Grand Universal Mind with all its parallels!—the "Mighty Oz!"...so to speak. Dreams or *death* is the *only way* to break free of these fleshly bonds that hold us. Our psyches, quite literally, are imprisoned until "death do us part" at which point this Energy / Spirit, together with all its images, memories and sounds is forever freed and allowed to roam the Vastness of Space, the Great *un*-Create Eternal Sea!

I have previously spoken at length (sometimes ad nauseam et ad Infinitum) about the theory of "ghostly sightings," particularly *ghosts* who appear dressed in "period costumes;" for instance, a woman wandering down a corridor wearing a long, flowing nightgown and carrying a candle-stick. She is disturbed not even *one jot* by her environment. (Namely by us with mouths agape who are staring at her!) This may be nothing more than a *holographic 3-D image* of that person caught in a time warp *of her own particular period!* (Say, for instance, the 18th century.) Maybe she was on her way to the bathroom, aka "the water closet." After all, why would a ghost be wearing clothes anyway? Even the Great Cosmos Itself has a memory which, just like our own mini-mental computers, is chock-full-of sounds and pictures. There is some amazing process out there in the Ether (don't ask me what!) by which all activity—animal, vegetable and mineral—is accurately recorded.

We, as individual parts of the Great Musical Vibrational Universe, are basically single musical notes meant to resonate harmoniously within the Symphonic Whole. Some of us, unfortunately being somewhat *dissonant*, create chaos by our blundering cacophonous sojourn through this existence sometimes laughingly referred to as "life."

Yet when we resonate together, as a Whole (note), this then is a beautiful thing. For one (Cosmic) moment the world is at *peace*.... And at that precise, precious moment when we are *all One*, it is then we practicing psychics are able to pluck from the Universe pictures, sounds and thoughts from long ago, the present or from the far distant future because All Is One and One is All, Forever and Ever unto Eternity.

If we are to believe that an event (say, 9/11) can be foretold, then it follows that no one or no-thing can change the outcome of that "program," so to speak. It is destined to unfold *exactly as it was meant to unfold*, whether a psychic, seer or prophet was present to witness it *in his Mind's Eye*, or not!

For *"those in the know"* (namely psychic people), the outcome of absolutely everything is pre-*determined* and there is no such thing as Free Will! Either you are pregnant or you are not! No such thing as *nearly pregnant.* You cannot have it both ways. Either positively there is free will or no free will and everything is pre-ordained.

They say (whoever "they" are) that the psychological consequences on the individual psyche—if the future was ABSOLUTELY KNOWN TO HIM FOR *CERTAIN* AND IT WAS FOR CERTAIN ACTUALLY REVEALED *TO HIM*—would be horrifying and nerve-racking, as would be the lives of his clients, friends and family to whom he must tell all, or just simply—lie!

Dreadful events such as excruciating physical pain, loss of worldly goods, unwanted years of lonely, loveless and sexless monotony, hopelessness; death of loved ones and, finally, to know the exact day, hour and moment of *your own demise* which may be *quick* (mercifully), but *more than likely* slow and agonizing....

"They" say it would turn existence into an endless nightmare of "waiting...waiting for the other shoe to drop!" Praying and faith would mean absolutely nothing (and they *don't*, in my opinion). Catastrophic!—would be the effect on the world in the face of unyielding uncertainty of all philosophies and religions. All the great books of "wisdom" would be annihilated in one swell swoop! Their use terminated!

Yes, staggering would be the practical consequences and the spiritual and philosophical implications of a future (already) "carved in stone." There are genuine skeptics whom I respect, but there are also envious scoffers who belong to a world-wide organization known as CSI-COP (Commitee for Scientific Investigation into Claims of the Paranormal), a group of mostly failed wannabe magicians who can't stand anyone making a living doing something they themselves have always wanted to do; which is odd, since most of them don't know the difference between slight-of-hand "magic" parlor tricks "for entertainment purposes only" and *true* psychic journeys into the realm of the Electrical / Spiritual, Fourth dimension.

Under the guise of scientific investigation, CSICOP states that "If psychics can see the future, why then don't they warn the world of impending disasters, such as 9/11?" To which my rejoinder is always: "We do, and did—in all the major newspapers—but nobody listened. And they never will. Because even that *(to not listen)* is also already fated!"

The future *is carved* in stone—including WW III!—and nothing but *nothing* can be done to change, alter or prevent it except the intervention of the Star-travelers / God / *Yahweh*—whatever! Only when they return will the world be at peace…. So, if it's true that "it would be nerve-wracking to know the future for certain"—well, let me say this—they're right! It is! I know, because I live it every day!… Che sera, sera.

The free world must contend with North Korea and then by extension, Red China! Sooner rather than later, when they are more powerful and more deadly!

OSAMA BIN LADEN, or more probably his remains, will be brought to the U.S. to be tried (postumously) for the worst war crime in the history of the world! Hanged, drawn-and-quartered, beheaded, disemboweled—after which a suitable punishment should then be considered.

Cosmic Catastrophe!

A great comet – not yet observed by astronomers – is on a collision course with **Earth**! However a slight deviation from its natural elliptic orbit will miraculously spare us the horror of being slammed into oblivion! Bouncing off the surface of our atmosphere as a stone skips over a pond, it returns to deep space whence it came (…this time). Yet in its wake – disaster! Earthquakes – the likes of which have never been seen! Mountain high tidal waves will engulf entire cites and forests! New coast lines! Up is down – and down is up! This great cosmic interloper comes round but once every million years or so – so thank your lucky stars (no pun intended) that you won't be very young when next it does.

Beautiful **Hawaiian Islands Restaurant,** nestled among cloud-shrouded mountains – suddenly plunges! Many die.

Violent street gangs – worldwide – are broken up by the army. Brought before the courts, thugs are given a choice: "sign up for five or sign *off for ten"* (– in the **Big House,** that is).

Beware the return of **Mikail** "Mark of the Beast" **Gorbachev!** His newspaper column, as it appeared in the June 17, 2007 Toronto Star, is overtly a call for peace but hides the real agenda: – a slow, but sure grab for world power. Remember the old USSR motto? – "two steps forward, one step back!"

A major **North American City** legally sanctions the first **Euthanasia Center**. (New York? Toronto? Montgomery? Alabama?)

An allegedly recently discovered manuscript, purportedly penned by the long departed "seer of seers" **Michel de Nostradame (Nostradamus),** in which new prophecies that purport to peer much further into the future than does the original **MILLENNIUM,** is revealed to be fake and shall be discarded as such, along with its author.

The Extraterrestrials who created us halt the carnage when they return to establish world peace. With their *return* comes the inevitable "re-thinking" of *all* world religions as we realize that *these* Beings *are* the gods to whom we have genuflected and worshiped, all these **millennia.**

An iron-fisted Russian dictator unites the disparate **Balkan States** to raise once again the powerful "hammer & sickle" – the **USSR!**

U.S. President **GEORGE W. BUSH** is struck by lightning not far from the **White House**. (A lightning strike, stroke, bullet – or just wishful thinking?) after which he lights up like a sparkler on the Fourth of July!

A jetliner with blue/red stripes crashes head-long into the tower of a major Airport! Impact pulps everything and all! Terrible! Awful! (Perhaps from **India**?)

STONEHENGE, England's most lucrative tourist trap, becomes one of the many landing sites of Extraterrestrials when they return, en masse.

PRESIDENT BUSH and fanatical evangelists – especially "born again" nut bars – bring the plagues of Egypt to North America. The more these bible-thumpers come to idolize Bush the more they doom the U.S. and the rest of the world to darkness, locust, boils, rivers of blood and the "death of every first born." (Let's hope Bush is the eldest.)

Former New York mayor **RUDY GIULIANI** couldn't get elected dog catcher, much less President of these United States. He's too mean-spirited. And besides, he probably doesn't even like animals (dogs, cats) and everybody knows you can't trust anyone who doesn't like animals.

After the reign of Canadian Prime Minister **STEPHEN HARPER,** comes a female P.M. However that is some time off since Mr. Harper shall "sit" for at less two-a-half terms.

Water is so scarce in so many U.S. cities that America will make an attempt to surreptitiously siphon off entire lake systems from its favorite neighbor to the north, which is to say – us! However Canada, always willing to compromise, strikes a deal with Washington in that cross border restrictions regarding taxes on trade goods are relaxed.

General obesity in America and Canada reaches such pandemic levels that the government is forced to investigate food sources in order to reverse the trend.

Domestic violence in North America homes increases exponentially as families fail to cope with the ever-rising costs of living. When the all-powerful Yankee dollar reaches Monopoly money value – all hell breaks loose! (Indeed, Monopoly money may well become *more* valuable than so-called *legal tender!*)

Russian President **VLADIMIR PUTIN** begins the job of reuniting the **USSR** but is pushed aside by one who makes this current leader look like Little Lord Fauntleroy. He is *that* ferocious! Then *he* will team with Red China, possibly Korea. World – watch out!

The absolutely positive 1890's identity of London's "**JACK THE RIPPER**" comes uncovered as having been either a Freemason or a member of the *Plymouth Brethren* (COB – Church of the Brethren), whose mission in life allegedly was – *and is* – to destroy prostitutes and anything this cult deemed "unclean."

The great bridge to be destroyed by a force that shakes its very foundation. Two moons – blue moon – will then be visible.

POPE BENEDICT – believe it or not – slips on a banana peel while strutting down the Vatican steps and snaps his spine like a twig. Looking heavenward he is heard to exclaim: "Where is God when you need 'Em?"

U.S. President **GEORGE W. BUSH** – while in office or *not* – is shot point blank in the derrière, according to my **ass-trological** calculations. **INDIA** sees the costliest and deadliest train crash in that country's history which already boasts a superb "track" record of train wrecks. Takes place up a mountain – and on the ground! Two in one.

As in days of yore, when **Kings** and **Pharaohs** "employed" food-tasters for every meal, it once again becomes the norm as world-wide intelligence proves terrorist have infiltrated top chef positions.

JAMES T. WALSH, Sodus Point, N.Y. Representative loses his political clout (and maybe his freedom) when they discover millions missing from the post 9/11 disaster fund.

While the **IRAQ** war rages out of control, it becomes necessary to build internment camps as the only means of keeping citizens safe, since these so-called "**terrorist**" – cowards, all! – attack *only* unarmed civilian's, woman and children instead of *real* men – soldiers! – soldiers who can fight back!

Ex Vice-President **AL GORE** slips in the shower and is rushed to hospital where on entry all cameras follow him in this most embarr-*ass*-ing moment. He'll be the *butt* of jokes for months.

FIDEL CASTRO DEAD! Has been for quite some time but a secret society has kept it on the Q.T. for obvious political reasons.

On or about the 9/11 anniversary, the Secret Service apprehends a suspicious looking tourist and hits the jackpot, finding him none other than **OSAMA bin LADEN** himself. Unable to resist gloating at Ground Zero, he is instantly recognized and seized. Unbridled hubris gives him rope enough to hang himself – literally!

Al'Qaeda targets a mega media edifice to wipe out all communications world-wide and panic the people. Simultaneously a satellite is destroyed but their objective is thwarted as CNN or one of the other major news networks saves the day. Some of its crew is honored with Purple Hearts or its equivalent and medals for bravery "above and beyond."

BLACK in the red?
I predicted **CONRAD BLACK'S** fall from grace (in print) several years ago which has unfortunately proved all too true. And yet his troubles are not over. New charges are filed against the British lord when police – on a tip – raid his home to find a virtual cornucopia of drugs and Colombians producing only the very finest grain of cocaine,

worth a fortune, even by Black's standards! It was to be sold on the *Black* market. (Nyuk, nyuk.)

During his sojourn in Japan, **U.S. PRESIDENT GEORGE BUSH** is slipped poison – intentionally or otherwise – survives, but pukes out his guts – all over the Japanese Prime Minister's shoes! Oh well, like father like son. (Same thing, more or less, happened to BUSH, SR.)

Two hundred Canadian Vandoos from Quebec's 22nd regiment shall meet their Maker in Afghanistan when security at the "in country" base is breeched and a truck full of explosives detonates with such force as to spew death throughout the camp – annihilating all. This marks the largest single massacre since Canada's entry into the war and causes the government to rethink its involvement – but alas, too late for the world at large.

A U.S. decision to turn 2,200 Iraqis – including Sunni groups such as the Revolution Brigade and Mujahedeen Army – into a security force shall return to haunt America's efforts to secure a democratic Iraq when yet another fanatic rises from this welter of humanity and incites all out civil war!

Japan's switch to jury style jurisprudence has comical results when the Japanese – with their phobia against public debate – halts the program in its tracks.

U.S. Scientist combine DNA from deceased military generals (e.g. "I shall return" MacArthur and "blood and guts" Patton) to create the *Super*soldier!... Maybe sort of a "I shall return for *your* blood and guts!" kind of Gestalt General?

Billowy white clouds over Portugal form a huge cross that people interpret as Christ's imminent return.

Presidential candidate **JOHN EDWARDS** to be outed for the hypocritical schmuck he is when his name tops the list in the **D.C.**

MADAM'S little – or should that be – BIG, black book! Yet his milk-sop, wimpy wife still won't leave him, which is to say, won't leave her meal ticket.

A government building in Ireland is attacked! Although at first deemed to be I.R.A., it's soon discovered that Eastern terrorists are responsible.

A suicide bomber is apprehended in Canada – triggering massive panic throughout the populations in Toronto, Vancouver and Halifax.

The shocking kidnapping takes place prior to *Guy Fawkes* day. A Royal victim of the highest aristocratic pedigree is found dead – murdered! – to the world's shock.

A thumbprint/fingerprint becomes necessary for all air travel. Trouble is, they can also be forged and sold on the black market, thereby increasing exponentially the paranoia throughout an already hysterical public.

Nations are stunned when Canada declares "prostitution legal!"

Terrible weather in Vancouver, B.C. leaves the *Lion's Head Bridge* in shambles, as powerful winds and rains devastate Canadian coastal towns.

Great sink holes suddenly engulf luxurious homes and hotels in and around Florida...as this wonderful vacation spot slowly returns to the sea.

The financial world is precariously balanced on the precipice of collapse! Worse than the "dirty 30's" – when at least the few who still possessed money, money that was then backed by the gold standard were considered solvent – this crash will render even the billions of *"pieces of paper"* floating around the world worthless, as entire civilizations frantically search for new currency.

Retro-fashions the world over return to the '60s *look*: – sack dress, shameez, Naru jackets, etc. ...It's about time!

Cross-border smuggling of Mexicans and sundry will cease when the two hemispheres are One.

Buffalo and ostrich meat become main sources of protein for carnivores (us) as Mad Cow and Mad Chicken fears increase!

Aspartame, the substitute sweetener, to be officially removed from the marketplace by the F.D.A. as a carcinogen.

The world is going to the dogs—literally! More and more people, particularly the white races (Anglo Saxons, Swedes, Danish, etc), will be choosing pets (dogs, cats) over the often thankless job of raising children. In the coming years you will hear women (and men) referring to their four-legged progeny, thus: "Come on, kids" or, "How are my babies doing today?" or—and most sickening of all —"Come give momma a big kiss!"...Yuk! Gag me with a spoon! Meanwhile Chinese, Arabs, Greeks and Italians will con*tinue to breed like minks.*

Italy's Mt. Vesuvius suddenly erupts with enough force to be heard around the world! Many, many killed!

As stated in my 1975 predictions, "Peoples of the world shall move from the extreme *white* and the extreme *black* to the middle mellow blend of café' au lait and racism shall be no more." Remember: It takes both the *white* keys *and* the *black* keys to make beautiful music.

Like an elevator car whose cable *snaps* at the hundred floor level, North American real estate plummets! People with only a few dollars will be able to buy whole blocks of houses and commercial properties, that is if the present currency is still worth anything, since monies the world over will be useless without the gold standard behind it. The next "coin of the realm" may very well be bottle caps! The Canadian dollar isn't worth much more than that, anyway.

A giant meteor or comet, tracked by observatories world-wide! All eyes riveted to see "where on Earth" (literally) it slams! I believe somewhere in the Rockies, which explains the above predictions thereto of wide spread fire and destruction!

"Necessity is the mother of invention," goes the adage. Therefore I predict a Super Microchip to hit the world market in answer to skyrocketing gas prices! Since a future "seven dollars a liter" per gallon price tag at the pumps is quite likely, this Wonder Chip will be built into new cars and easily placed in existing ones. Requiring recharging (with a "new energy source") only about once a month, it will render all fossil fuels obsolete. *Much* blood will be spilled before this transition is complete.

Although the American dollar loses ground, it shall remain the world's strongest currency; which is to say: whoever carries the biggest stick wields the financial power. As far as I know, it still is and will continue to be — AMERICA!

No doubt exists in my Mind's Eye that we are headed for a cashless society!

After all, what good is wealth if you can't flaunt it, if all you can pull out of your pocket is thin air. Hell, I can do that now, and I'm broke!

Don't trust the Euro. When the Mideast and Europe blow — so will it!

The coming real estate and cash crash makes the Dirty '30's Depression look like a Sunday school picnic! Although a few may possess "money," a dollar without the gold-standard is just worthless paper! Not worth the *one hundred pennies* it was during the Depression Era, *with* the gold behind it. No gold equals worthless paper; ergo, the "wealthy" will be as *poor* as the poor! (Chew on that a while!)

When "strategic" nuclear bombing begins—all is lost! To be avoided at all cost, *lest it costs all!!!*

I have prophesied countless times—beware Russia!... Remember their motto: "two steps forward, one step back." More than ever the former USSR is now confused, but should these disparate countries unite under a strong dictator—watch out!

Red China aligns itself with one or more of the Mideast countries, possibly India, before moving out against the West. Either way India becomes all-powerful over the next few years, but in the end, she *will* do the right thing.

The air in major cities becomes polluted to the point that people (of "means") will have to rent metered oxygen tanks from the government....Fifty cents per average breath, one dollar per deep gasp! Talk about "owning the air we breath!"

Many Americans will immigrate to Canada as both political and natural climates change drastically! Particularly, large numbers will move steadily toward the climes of northern Ontario and the Northwest Territories (NWT) in search of fresh-air and wide open spaces!

As always when war is imminent, every aspect of the entertainment industry benefits: — movies, television, live theatre, mime — you name it, it prospers, as people seek any form of *escape* from life's harsh realities. Unfortunately drugs and booze — *booze the most powerful drug of all!* —will flourish!

Prince Edward's *flouncing* becomes too much for the already scandal-ridden British Monarchy when the failed British Marine is caught on camera in *fag*-rante delicto —(by the paparazzi, no less)— cavorting about in full la femme regalia. Truly an outfit fit for a *(drag)* queen!

Princess Diana's body to be exhumed either for relocation or another post-mortem because of ongoing rumors surrounding her sudden, violent death!

Royal rebel pain-in-the-butt **Sarah "Fergie" Ferguson** is fishing for a new husband-slash-lover! Oddly enough, *fishing* is the operative word here! I predict during a sojourn at a resort (of sorts) where fishermen abound, the former **Mrs. Prince Andrew** will meet Mr. Right and simply *reel* him in. Start *trolling*, Fergie Darling, start *trolling*. The lure is set and the bait — is you!

I see battleships, fighter planes, ICBMs (Intercontinental Ballistic Missiles) surrounding New Zealand and Australia — poised for trouble! The word *Anzus* comes to mind: "the alliance formed between Australia, New Zealand and the U.S. (1951) to protect those countries in the Pacific from armed attack!"

During the administration of former U.S. President George Bush, *Sr.*, **I correctly prophesied** an assassination attempt. Unfortunately I still see the funeral caisson trundling down Pennsylvania Avenue.

California will *not* suffer a catastrophic earthquake in the near future, but in Boston I see **walls of fire!**

A devastating explosion destroys large portions of Las Vegas!

Because of terrorism fears, **American** and **Canadian** inner cities will adopt a police state-like army to protect the citizens as violent crime increases.

Except in real estate, there will be a vigorous upswing in the world economy over the next three years, particularly in Canada, the U.S., Great Britain and France where literally *billions* of dollars will pour in from **BIG TIME GAMBLING and ENTERTAINMENT!!!** "Toronto the good" becomes "Toronto where the action *is good!*"

Welcome To The 51St State: Canada Continues to be (defacto) annexed by the U.S., as I predicted twenty years ago in the *Toronto Star*. I also said: "Quebec attempts to secede amid bloody border skirmishes." These issues will be revisited.

VIOLENCE! BLOODY VIOLENCE! Around media mogul **Conrad Black** and his wife, former *Toronto Sun* columnist **Barbara Amiel.**

Watch out! The appearance of Gorbachev ("Mark of the Beast") and Boris Yeltsin in Canada simultaneously. This juncture in space, time and history did mark the countdown to Armageddon. President Putin may very well be the trigger. The guy is a lunatic! Remember Russia's policy for world domination: **"two steps forward, one step back."**

Return of **"The Mark of the Beast!"** Gorbachev cometh again!

Prince Andrew ascends the throne sometime during this decade.

The **British Royal Family** experiences three personal tragedies of epic proportions.

Soldiers with the **"red star"** on their helmets overrun Eastern European borders.

World War III looms! The yellow horde crosses the Yangtze and the **blue-turbaned madman** rises from the East.

Gold standard increases threefold in a useless attempt to shore up equally useless paper money.

Mankind's only hope to escape extinction is to colonize other planets. The good earth is doomed! Even when the Star-travelers return to halt the horror—peace, at best, is temporary — a thousand years. ("...and I shall create for you a new Heaven and a new Earth.")

Christian Bible

The Pope from the un-holy alliance shall be chased from the High place — to flee the turbaned madman! He shall *not* return and the Holy See shall be near the sea, land-locked on three sides.

Home-grown terrorists world-wide are "rooted" from their rat holes by "exterminators."

"Terrorist" is too good a word for "things" that are nothing more than snakes, rats and cockroaches with arms and legs. (Japanese forces who attacked Pearl Harbor were *real* terrorists—but at least had guts enough to wage war against armed men, not unarmed civilians in an office building filled with women and children!) Hard measures will be taken at home: suspected insurgents rounded up and interned.

"The sea [and the grave] shall give up their dead on the Great Day of Tribulation. Then shall there follow a **Golden Era**." [Revelations]: Probably through a highly advanced form of DNA engineering and the cloning of life's building blocks, the very essence of life that resides in the bones of the living and *the lo-o-ng dead*, the Star Traveling **Gods** will **resurrect** *t*he deceased as the living (the Elect) ascend to heaven…. ("Beam me up Scotty.")

Then shall there follow a **Golden Era, a thousand years of peace,** while **The Lord of Hosts** (which is to say, the Chief Extraterrestrial Astronaut) establishes his rule on Earth.

A theory that **Jesus Christ** *was* the first case of artificial (in vitro) fertilization will be proffered by someone other than me (for a change), and will be a respected member of the scientific community who *also* endorses my theory.

Popies will grow on the grave of WWII IWO JIMA hero IRA HAYES, an Arizona Pima tribe Native, to show the innocence of his soul.

Canadian Government radically reduces green house gas emissions while convincing **China** and **America** to do likewise. If not, the Arctic will melt and then we're *all* going to be in *biiiig* trouble.

Another liquor prohibition-type restriction will go into effect when **U.S. Government** bans booze because of exorbitant medical costs due to alcohol related illnesses. (Costs which Congress *has to pay* when it adopts its own socialized medical plan.)

I have predicted this for years: some day **HILLARY CLINTON** will be President of these United States of America with husband, **BILL**, as de facto President; a "two-for-one" deal.
Marriage becomes so obsolete that the only way to remember it?if it's ever remembered—will be through reading history books (or possibly on the net).

The toy industry is turned on its ear when consumer experts discover China is using garbage—waste materials—to produce toxic toys. Labor takes a nose-dive as the retail business pulls out until investigations are completed.

"In the coal mines of America, a monstrous *cover* comes to *light*, with the excavation of long gone tunnels, hidden beneath foliage *bright*. Over one hundred skeletons plus, pickaxes still in hand, were left to languish, suffer and fight, that cave-in when took place that night! Paid off and sworn to secrecy, all the town goes to *trial*, along with those "great" corporate *heads*, on *pikes* which will not see a smile." In short, they all get the *shaft*!"

A concrete causeway over the city of Toronto collapses! Bodies strewn everywhere!

Mafia mobs and other such groups will make organized sports nothing more than organized crime. (Is there *dis*-organized crime?) New guidelines are quickly put in place to keep it crime free.... After all, only the government is *allowed* to *steal honestly*. (How's that for an oxymoron?)

Science proves conclusively the beached whales phenomenon is directly due to "*sonar bleeps*" of ocean traffic which interfere with and confuse the electrical signals and impulses by which these great mammals communicate and navigate.... Think of commercial aircraft flying at high altitudes at night, during fierce electrical storms that interfere with and confuse its intricate and sensitive navigating equipment. Result?—CRASH!!! Ditto for humans with their sensitive elec-

trical circuitry: too much interference and overloading. Result?—
CRASH! Nervous breakdown!

Pollutants in the air and water are so toxic to everything and everyone that people under stress begin breaking out in horrific blistering
sores and boils that resemble the ancient Plagues of Egypt and so are
regarded as *evil* and therefore ostracized from the tribe of Man, as in
days of old.

The **NRA** again becomes a hot issue when yet another teen open fires
on students somewhere in Middle America (the initial "M" is prominent), this time by a teenage girl!

China suffers catastrophic floods, nearly wiping it out. (And that's saying a lot when you think of the staggering populations!) Eventually
the country amalgamates with and becomes subsumed by other nations and peoples, thus relinquishing the strong arm of dictatorship.

An *Olympic* catastrophe—literally!—when a Canadian contingent is
attacked by al-Qaida.

Democracy, as we in the West know it, will soon cease to exist. "We
the people, by the people, for the people" is a mantra lost to the next
generation. If *"choosing"* no longer seems to work, perhaps a "tyrant"
would? (Whoops!—nearly forgot—we already have one!)

New Orleans experiences so much lawlessness, murder and general
mayhem that the city, literally under siege from within, declares a
State of Emergency—and Martial Law as residents flee for their lives!

RED CROSS organization is caught with its hand in the cookie jar
when millions—if not billions—are discovered in offshore accounts,
around the world. This scandal is worthy of the *Guinness Book of
World Records*! A black day and a black mark against world charities!

Tobacco companies are finally outlawed, paving the way for the incredibly lucrative black market trade. Violent gun battles of the early liquor prohibition era will erupt like Mt. Vesuvius (which, by-the-bye, is also set to blow). Ironically, marijuana becomes legal!

Because of ozone depletion, parts of America that rarely see rain are inundated!.... Great floods reminiscent of the Biblical deluge *will be common* and widespread. (The *Grand Canyon* once again becomes the ocean floor.) We have pretty much destroyed Mother Earth and she in turn shall destroy us as a dog shakes off its fleas. Water and fire! —and...how long can you tread water?

Russian President **VLADIMAR PUTIN** has a change of heart, suddenly turning against U.S. President **GEORGE BUSH**. America feels the wrath of the *new* Soviet Union (USSR).

U.S. Showbiz:

JOAN RIVERS: Tragedy strikes when a puddle of plastic is discovered poolside near the spot where the subcutaneous "queen of cutting wit" *should* have been! Probably melted after dozing under the hot California sun – the result of too many plastic surgeries. The "**Fellowship of Plastic Surgeons of America**" posthumously bestows an award (probably also plastic) for meritorious selflessness in keeping so many doctors employed, surpassing even the record held by her comedic colleague **PHILLIS DILLER**, who, by the bye, is very much intact and still on the earth plane. (Probably held together with *Crazy Glue!*) Well, we all know Hollywood people are … plastic?

Celebrity bounty hunter **DUANE "DOG" CHAPMAN** continues to have hard luck simply because there is something inherently repugnant about people who hunt down people for money. (Even though we all somehow have to make a living.) Eventually this celebrity stalker will end up back in the Big House, for such is his nature. And woe unto him should he be incarcerated with some of the people he has already helped send up!

Infamous "les"-be (girl) friends iconoclast **ROSIE O' DONNELL** admits publicly that being nasty is due to being nasty-lookin' and fat! An' that's that! After an on air nervous break down – even **DONALD "THE TRUMP"** may come to her rescue.

HEATHER MILLS, ex-squeeze of **PAUL Mc CARTNEY** (poster boy for "there ain't no fool like an old fool" and who is now enlightened of his decades old question: "Will you still want me, will you still need me, when I'm 64?") – will unfortunately lose her other limb to the same disease that claimed the other. Without a leg to stand on, I'm sure she'll attract yet another horny billionaire who gets off on such things.

Lusty busty **DOLLY PARTON** (the "Working From Nine To Five" gal) is discovered at her passing to be hermaphroditic! Ergo, the country singing diva probably never did have that famous bust reduction but simply exchange them for smaller ones.

SHARON STONE (*Fatal Instinct, Casino*) will suffer three major strokes, the fatal third!

OPRAH at deaths door! Too many "yo yo" diets dangerously deplete her body of potassium. A serious heart arrhythmia problem strikes the *Color Purple* star who's then rushed to hospital where the purple of her lips returns to healthy pink.

OPRAH to pass? After falling off her wallet and breaking her leg, peritonitis sets in and the talk-show diva ascends to that great television set in the sky…. It's the first time in history that anyone will die from too much money… (except for King Midas).

"PARTY" PARIS HILTON finesses her way back into law and order, but it won't be long 'til she returns to old haunts and habits. But the poor little rich girl is going to have an epiphany …. While aboard a great white yacht with a wild party in progress, this floating palace suddenly tilts, founders – then sinks! (Shades of the **TITANIC!**) Frantically struggling to stay afloat, "tiltin" Hilton is rescued by a quick thinking – tall, dark and handsome young man who either observed the tragedy from shore or was also on board. Either way, Paris truly finds God, a husband and the one who will save her from herself. ("…You are responsible for the life you save.")

Old Chinese Proverb.

WHOOPI GOLDBERG is offered the role of a lifetime: playing the voice and face of **Snoopy,** of cartoon character fame **PEANUTS.** Although perhaps at first offended, she shouldn't *turn her nose up at this idea.*

KIRSTY ALLEY loses the **JENNY CRAIG** throne for being too fat to fit! She begins a new career, touring with **BARNUM & BAILEY** and **CONKLIN SHOWS CIRCUS'** as the featured "**FAT LADY.**"

KEITH RICHARDS, after his foray into acting with *Pirates Of The Caribbean,* starring **JOHNNY DEPP,** is bitten by the bug and becomes a *geri*-actor star. The aging musician and actor forms his own production company, aptly named: Over The Hill Productions!

Vegas lounge lizard **WAYNE NEWTON** has had so many face lifts, eyelid and chin tucks that he's beginning to look Oriental.…As a matter of fact I predict this desert denizen will embark on a world tour which includes China and Japan where he'll be a huge smash, thereby satisfying a *yen.*

60-year-old "*Shark*" star **JAMES WOODS** dies in the throes atop his "baby" girlfriend, **ASHLEY MADISON.** It seems years of changing diapers and love-making will take its toll.

RYAN O"NEAL'S immune system is so over-taxed from all the stress (**FARRAH FAUCET,** troubled son, **REDMAN,** etc.), that the one-time boxer is literally courting his own doom! Tired and worn out, this fine actor will succumb to the next onslaught.

O.J. stealthily returns to the world as a successful murder mystery writer! – attracting a whole new generation of fans. (Gee, I wonder where he gets his ideas from?)

Not to be outdone by this new master of the macabre, actor **ROBERT BLAKE** – famous for his erstwhile starring movie role of **TRUMAN CAPOTE'S** novel "**In Cold Blood!**" and now *infamous* for the acquittal of murdering his wife, **BONNIE BLAKE** – now teams with **SIMPSON** and together will co-write screenplays based on O.J.'S successful slash 'n' gash books which will also see unprecedented profits! (…There just ain't no justice at all!)
DANNY BONADUCHE ('70's hit series *The Partridge Family*) reinvents himself yet again after splitting from his manager wife who allegedly is having an affair with another – *woman?!* When he finally does kick the bottle, an entirely new career will beckon.

Former Gays – oops! – I mean *Grays Anatomy* actor **ISAIAH WASHINGTON** surprises the entertainment world when chosen as principle lead in an upcoming TV series based on gay rights and their communities worldwide… his "gay" faux pas notwithstanding.

Legendary "Golden 40's" actor **KICK DOUGLAS** (Father of Michael) shows no sign of slowing down or retiring as he turns out yet one more best-selling book about old Hollywood and garners another *best-supporting* Oscar for portraying himself in this, the story of his life. (… Hmm, not a bad title: "THE STORY OF HIS LIFE.")

Die Hard star **BRUCE WILLIS** gets tough with ex-wife **DEMI MOORE'S** toy boy lover, **ASTON KURCHNER.** In a "rit of jealous fage" he punches out the kid – then is charged with "assault against a minor" for which the *Children's Aid Society* steps in and sues the wannabe **HUMPHREY BOGARD** look-a-like for a million dollars on behalf of Kurchner. Remember, Brucey baby: – Ya' snooze ya' lose.

Caribbean Pirate **JOHNNY DEPP** finds himself immersed in a child custody battle because of his continuous absenteeism. He'll have to choose between a full-time career and his family or this profiteer, *Captain Jack Sparrow,* may find himself on the losing end of splitting his booty with his "better" half.... (And I mean "booty" in the old fashion sense of the word, not the new!) "Aye, Captain Sparrow, 'tis the dead that are the lucky ones." (from **ROBERT LOUIS STEVENSON'S** *Treasure Island.*)

"Today" anchor **MATT LAUER** risks loosing his job as his womanizing goes right off the charts! The top executives demand he start toeing the line – or else! Namely by setting *them* up with some of the broads from his *own* harem. (Or, at least, have the decency to air his scandalous behavior for all the world to see and enjoy! This would certainly ensure high ratings for the network.)
DR. PHIL is spotted at the *Playboy Mansion* having a *real* good time! Too good, in fact, for his wife **ROBIN** to overlook. It appears the "good" doctor is gonna need a good shrink, lest Robin flys the coop!... Physician, heal thyself.

VAL KILMER, formerly *Batman* but now known as *Fatman*, is suffering from excessive avoirdupois: – he's too damn fat! – and becomes America's spokesperson for "super fat celebrities needing help," slimming down to a mere shadow of his bloated self.

JUDGE JUDY enters politics and surprises everyone by winning – first time out. I see congress, the Senate Building (domed roof).

BRITNEY SPEARS temporarily loses custody of her children when she's found passed out in a famous hotel nightclub.... Heavy drug use suspected.

PRINCE CHARLES is plagued by health problems from waiting to long to ascend the British throne.... And never he shall.... Tragedy waits in the wings! Only **PRINCE ANDREW** will survive to rule.

QUEEN ELIZABETH'S husband, **PRINCE PHILIP** will inadvertently be responsible for yet one more juicy scandal to this Royal

House after which Her Majesty, too exhausted, abdicates, in one way or another. Yet I say again "neither Charles nor his prodigy shall rule. Only Andrew."

ANTONIO BANDERAS, fed up with his Peter Pan wife **MELANIE GRIFFEN'S** crazy antics and excessive plastic surgeries, temporarily leaves only to return to find her in the sack with the pool boy, which really *sinks* their marriage.

WHITNEY HOUSTON literally crawls back to **BOBBY BROWN** when her second shot at stardom turns to dust. She is found groping around her mansion confused and incoherent, to the point that even B.B. is disgusted.… What a shame for such a talent.

Super successful *Harry Potter* author **J.K. ROWLINGS** becomes a target of death threats from fundamental Christendom the world because of her books "magic" themes. Forced underground when a nut bar attempts to do her in (a la. **SALMAN RUSHDIE'S** *Satanic Verse*), some soul-searching by the famed writer brings her out of hiding and back into the fray, determined to stand her ground. She realizes this hatred has more to do with financial-envy than it has to do with "magic."… How Christian of them!

Ailing **FARRAH FAUCET** will find a miracle cure in Germany or Switzerland that costs her her fortune but saves her life!… Truly the adage "your money *or* your life" will never be more appropriate.

JOHN TRAVOLTA wins an Oscar for his "brilliant" portrayal of a fat singing/dancing **BARBRA STREISAND**-type character in *Hairspray*. By the same token his, uh, – *her* movie co-star, **CHRISTOPHER WALKIN,** garners a special award for demonstrating possibly the worst singing voice since late dancer **GENE KELLY,** who sounded like a cross between a rutting bull moose and "*The Godfather*" trying to croon.

SARAH JESSICA PARKER is destined to become an integral part of a great American Monument.... She's got a head that belongs on Mount Rushmore.

Mount Rushmore, famous for its granite-jawed giant busts of four U.S. Presidents **(George Washington, Thomas Jefferson, Abraham Lincoln and Theodore Roosevelt)**, will suffer serious disfigurement, either natural, or man-made. (Terrorist activity?) Perhaps **SARAH JESSICA PARKER'S** head is just too much for them!

JANE FONDA, acting icon and often rebel *with a cause*, to be stricken by deadly viral respiratory infection. Although touch and go, she recovers completely.

With respect to our acutely brunette complected brothers and sisters, Hollywood is becoming keenly aware of the opportunity in-equities in the film industry. Therefore with this in mind, I predict a remake of several former blockbuster movies with an all-black cast. They have already retooled the *WIZARD OF OZ* as "THE WIZ" and the classic *SUNSET BOULEVARD* starring **DIANNE CARROLL.** Future send-ups will be *BATMAN* as "BLACKMAN" and *APOCALYPSE NOW* as a "PACK-O-LIPS NOW" —soon to be followed by many others.

KRAFT DINNER, the staple of all starving musicians, writers and actors (*before* they made it big—and even sometimes after!) will receive the equivalent of an Oscar or a Lifetime Achievement Award. For without its existence many successful performing artists whom we love and admire today, probably would not be here. To succeed in this business, one must be *Krafty.* (Nyuk, Nyuk!)

LUCIANO PAVAROTTI, perhaps the greatest operatic voice of the last half-century (with the possible exception of the late **MARIO LANZA),** will be stilled. Yet his legacy will live on through a young lady of exceptional voice and beauty.

The popularity of the Kojak and Vin Diesel "chrome-dome look" quickly falls out of fashion as women are again attracted to lush, thick, wavy hair. Males living *on the fringe (pun intended)* of society will again desperately search for the ever-elusive elixir of (hair growing) life.

The hugely successful **Degrassi** television series, **Degrassi: The Next Generation, Degrassi High, Degrassi Talks** (*Degrassi Goes To Mars?! Degrassi Meets Abbott and Costello and The Wolfman!?*) is about to explode from mere stratospheric success to beyond thermospheric — *the highest of the high!* No word yet exists to describe the scope and magnitude of its coming success! Ineffable! — Imminent!!

Already viewed in every far flung corner of the world, probably even in Nunavut ("Eskimo" country) and the jungles of Borneo and translated into every language, no doubt probably including Swahili and Inui ("Eskimo"), I predict **Degrassi** will eventually replace **Anne of Green Gables** as the international favorite, weaving its way into the cultural fabric of our hearts and souls.

For executive producers -slash- co-founders of **Epitome Pictures**, **Linda Schuyler and Stephen Stohn** will enjoy yet greater success, soon garnering Oscars. Okay folks — center stage!

MADONNA, looking a "little long in the tooth" these days (not to mention long in the butt!), will *(should)* hang up her spandex pants before she becomes the laughing stock of showbiz, as the "world's oldest sex symbol." Packaging, promoting and producing talent will make her successful, far more than did her own stage career.

Celebrity deaths — ladies first: **LAUREN BACALL,** former British Prime Minister **MARGARET "IRON LADY" THATCHER, JACK** (*The Odd Couple*) **KLUGMAN, MOHAMMED ALI,** former U.S. Presidents **JIMMY CARTER** and **GERALD FORD, EARNEST BORGNINE** (*Marty, McHale's Navy*), **RICHARD WIDMARK** (The Alamo) and, to insure equality of the races, thespian **SYDNEY PORTIER** and Canadian jazz great **OSCAR PETERSON.**

TV talk-show host **DR. PHIL,** who preaches interminably about the virtues of "loving yourself as you are," undergoes a series of micro-hair transplants that end up rendering his head a second cousin to a chia pet! (Probably "hates himself as he is.")

As **MARTIN LANDAU** was to **BELLA LUGOSI,** earning him an Oscar for his eerie portrayal of the late **Dracula** actor, so will **MATT DILLON** be to equally late horror-meister **BORIS KARLOFF** (Frankenstein's Monster!). Dillon is called upon to play both Karloff and his alter ego —*"The Monster!"* This establishes him as the great character actor I know him to be. At first he balks (naturally), but I predict that if he takes on this project the *You, Me and Dupree* star will go on to enjoy a long and illustrious career. (Psst.! — Mr. Dillon... do not make the same mistake Mr. Lugosi did when he refused the role of "The Monster." He forever regretted it!)

BARBARA AMIEL, wife of beleaguered media mogul **CONRAD BLACK** (— whoops! — I meant to say, **"Lord Black of Crossharbour"**... "tut-tut, old man... please pass the snuff," and all that rot), was once a lowly columnist with the *Toronto Sun.* Barbara should bone up on her typing, because I predict sooner or later she'll be right back where she started. "What goes around comes around," and one should *never* but never forget one's roots.

"Controlling" **TOM CRUISE,** which he is often referred to by various ladies, is producing a big budget horror flick. Indeed, it'll be the biggest Hollywood horror flick since *Plan 9 From Outer Space* was voted by the Motion Picture Academy as the worst movie ever produced in the past half-century, winning its director, **ED WOOD,** an Oscar (posthumously). Not to be outdone, Cruise's Magnum Opus will equal (quite possibly surpass) that "distinction." It'll be a case of one-downmanship. The audience will be mesmerized with their *"eyes wide shut."* (Or is that *eyes shut tight!*) He'll have them in the aisles — leaving!

BO DEREK, beautiful svelte star of "10" and widow of 1940's handsome hunk-turned-director, **JOHN DEREK (*Knock On Any Door*,**

HUMPHREY BOGART), is going to need one *(a derrick, that is)* just to move around! But more than that I "see" lots of blood surrounding the now reclusive actress. She must take great care about whom she allows in her home. Blood!-Blood!-Blood! — everywhere!! (Or perhaps just a scene from her next movie.)

REGIS PHILBIN *(LIVE with REGIS and KELLY)* is charged with sexual improprieties when one of the show's co-host hopefuls is passed over in favor of another. "Hell hath no furry!"— etc.. When Philbin gets through these troubles his health will deteriorate to the point where he'll die on camera for all the world to see! The upside is with so many facelifts he'll look great in "the box." But if he has anymore work done — and already his face looks like his pigtails are too tight — he'll be wearing his bellybutton between his eyes! (And I do realize that this is *stretching* the point.)

IVANA TRUMP, *GLOBE* advice columnist and former main squeeze of hotel mogul **DONALD TRUMP,** should run — not walk — to the to the nearest doctor who will order for her a complete MRI, even if she has to pay for it herself (which of course, she will, since this *is* the U.S. of A., and not Canada). There are lumps and bumps in her body that quick action will prevent from spreading, thereby saving her life! Pirates of the Caribbean star **JOHNNY DEPP** may have more in common than he thinks with real life Captain Blackbeard, the notorious American Pirate after whom Depp partly modeled his character, Captain Jack Sparrow. Blackbeard was finally killed in 1718 by the British Navy.... I sense the same tragedy may befall Depp through a bizarre accident during filming, something not unlike the beheading death of the late **VIC MORROW** who died while making *Twilight Zone: the movie.* (He saved two children before succumbing.) This is definitely not the way to get *a-head* in the biz.

TV talk show host **MONTEL WILLIAMS** to suffer fatal (or near fatal) heart attack! So crippling that retirement is imminent—perhaps even to that great "rocking chair in the sky!" ...I *see* boxing, should he survive. ...Exercise, maybe?

Hot young beauty **SCARLETT JOHANSSON** *(Match Point, Scoop)* is in grave danger of committing — or being involved in — vehicular manslaughter! The two words have just now struck my psyche! I *see* a red convertible sports car occupied by her and current beau, **JOSH HARTNETT,** speeding down a coastal road…. Easy does it now, e-e-easy does it…. (Again, perhaps just another scene from yet another movie.)

WOODY ALLEN, although every man's favorite neurotic (with whom most of us can identify), must be extremely careful about "falls" (and I don't mean Niagara); after all, he is at that critical age! I see a broken arm, possibly a concussion. (Or if he's lucky, perhaps merely a small stroke!) But that aside, the next three years should be incredibly successful for old four-eyes—the best of his career, and that's saying a lot!

MICKEY ROURKE, bad boy/tough guy *(Sin City Star)*, will make at least one more trip to the altar, even after two failed marriages — no, not to attend his own funeral but to tie again the matrimonial knot with a petite, auburn beauty who will bear him three children; two boys, a girl. (I suppose one *could* argue there's scant difference between weddings and funerals!) Even though his own childhood left much to be desired, I think he'll make a great father.
Movie genius **STEVEN SPIELBERG** produces and directs the life story of late, legendary horror master **BORIS KARLOFF** *(and his alter ego* **FRANKENSTEIN**). He'll have a difficult time choosing to cast either ROLLING STONES' **KEITH RICHARDS** (who already looks half-dead but doesn't have the good sense to lie down) and *You, Me and Dupree* star **MATT DILLON,** although I'm reasonably certain Dillon will get the nod if for no other reason than he appears to be "better fed" than does Richards and so will be judged to survive, at least until filming is through. Either way, the story will be told!

JENNIFER LOPEZ *swings* back to the musical side of her many major talents, preferring to concentrate her energies on jazz. Jennifer or "Jenny," which—according to the unabridged Oxford English Dictionary means "a female donkey or *ass*" (—and she certainly has plenty of that), will garner a Grammy or its equivalent for a jazzology CD. Kudos on her.

The Sopranos` star **JAMES GANDOLFINI** has a knee injury which is keeping him on the sidelines. I predict the TV godfather will gain enough weight as to warrent serious health problems! He's gonna throw his weight around—literally. Some of his "business associates" should "make him an offer he can't refuse," like go on a diet and start exercising. People are already referring to him as the *Slobfather!* — behind his back, of course.

DIANA ROSS, former SUPREMES singer and Academy Award Winner (for her portrayal of Billy Holliday in *Lady Sings The Blues*), is in grave danger of being roasted! No, not like the erstwhile hugely successful 70's TV show **CELEBRITY ROAST** — but a real-life, potentially deadly fire! I'm afraid Ms. Ross will backslide. Old (bad) habits die hard, possibly falling asleep in bed with a cigarette in her hand, or something equally deadly. I doubt she'll last much longer, but will first pen a best-selling autobiography.

The View co-host **BARBARA WALTERS** suffers debilitating face shingles. Doctors first suspect a stroke but soon realize it's the former. While convalescing, however, she does stroke out! — a stroke of luck, that is. A well-known publishing house advances her a king's ransom for her memoirs, to be made into a movie in which the old broad herself gets to do a walk-on. Barbara's thoughts turn from her lovelife to the *afterlife* as she desperately searches the Bible for loopholes after years of *dissing* (dis-respecting) nearly everyone!

UMA THURMAN and **JOHN TRAVOLTA** join forces in an upcoming comedic romp about gay-lesbian wrestling tag-teams who take on space aliens! This film, probably entitled **OUT OF THIS WORLD** (not to mention out of the closet!), will be executively produced by the estate of late Scientology guru, **L. RON HUBBARD.**

The *horrible hobby* of visiting the graves of the "rich and famous" (Princess Diana, John F. Kennedy, Marilyn Monroe, etc.) through the popular website: findagrave.com, set up by **JIM TIPTON** of Salt Lake City, is becoming so popular with necrophiles and macabre-seekers that it won't be long until innovators begin poking microscopic lenses through graves and crypt walls to sell weirdos a few moments privilege of seeing their favorite dead stars slowly rot! (...Don't look so shocked! The church already condones this gawking spectacle. For a "donation" they will put on display a *"relic,"* an appendage, such as a skeletal finger, hand or foot — and sometimes an entire body! — of some long dead "saint" in front of which the masses may genuflect and generally pay homage.... unless they have a *bone* to pick!

Busty, lusty singer **DOLLY PARTON** to contract rare lung disease requiring massive doses of steroids that cause her to bloat like the Hindenburg. For a while she'll look more like DOLLY *porpoise* than Parton but soon returns to normal when she's weened from the drugs. If lovable old comic **JERRY LEWIS** can do it, so can she. (... By the way, Jerry will soon pass.)

JERRY SPRINGER, TV talk-show host gauche, dies horribly (depending on your point of view) at the hands — and feet! — of a dozen or so guests during the *live* taping of an experimental show gaged to test the effects of alcohol on people over the course of an hour's drinking, as they hurl insults at one another. Suddenly blaming Springer for their woes (drunks and druggies have to blame someone!), they turn on the syndicated sex maniac and do him in!
EDDIE MURPHY and **MELANIE BROWN** ("Scary Spice" of the ex-girl band **SPICE GIRLS***)* are going to need a *band-aid to hold together* their new marriage as they start singing "the wedding bell blues," which is no mean feat since she can't carry a tune in a bucket! Felicitations flag when nuptials fail and this union ends in a flash! — even before the ink dries on the license. Meanwhile, cross-dressing hookers console Mr. Murphy at the end of a tedious day.

KEENEN IVORY WAYANS may be *smarting* over the final divorce settlement for ex-wife **DAPHNE,** but he'll be "laughing all the way to the bank" (to steal a line from the late **LIBERACE***)* when he turns his marriage-divorce story into an uproarious comedy.... Fear not, Keenen, you'll recoup everything — and more.

The next "greatest scandal of all time" coming down the pike — the first being the Da Vinci Code theory that **JESUS CHRIST** may have been human or at least half-human (a demigod) — shall be that SCIENTOLOGY founder **L. RON HUBBARD** was no more than a con-artist looking to make a quick buck—which he did! (And all the more power to him!) But I "see" something resembling a converted battleship — gun turrets and all! — "sailing the bounding main," with Hubbard as captain. (What the hell is a "bounding main," anyway?) Perhaps it's a film about his life, a kind of a modern day *Pirates Of The Caribbean* starring Captain Jack Sparrow—uh... I mean, Captain Hubbard. "Avast, ye` swabs!"

JIM CARREY will *never* tie the knot with **JENNY McCARTHY.** Similar to **JULIA ROBERT'S** character in *The Runaway Bride* (or something of that ilk), old Jim-bo will suddenly develop cold feet and flee for his life, always mindful that his *better half* could end up with the *better half* of his millions! This born out of fear that he could at any time slip back into that world of poverty which he knew so well as a child in Toronto, Canada, his home town. After the broken engagement, Jenny will not think Jimmy so jaunty.

ELLEN DEGENERES is worried sick she may lose her currant squeeze, **PORTIA De ROSSI,** to a man in the same manner she lost ex-squeeze **ANNE HECHE.** Not to worry, Ellen — because you will! I predict after losing two female lovers to men, the Emmy award-winning comic will give it a shot herself — wondering what all the fuss is about.... "Gee, maybe I'm missing out on something after all!" Big flash—you are! And you're gonna like it! Well, as the adaje goes: "Twice bitten thrice *guy!*"— and, "don't knock it till ya` try it!"

ROD STEWART, who now sounds like a croaking version of The Godfather: "...uhh, Santino, my son... I cut-ta you balls off!..." — etc., has to undergo more surgery to clear his throat. Miraculously the procedure succeeds, restoring him somewhat to his former self. "Do you think I'm sexy?"... Not right now Rod, but soon, very soon.

Talladega Nights star **WILL FERRELL** is one, miserable s.o.b. when not in the limelight. I predict young Will is gonna get himself stinkoed in a Los Angeles bar and, like many top funnymen who use comedy to compensate for their congenitally depressive personalities and general sense of self-loathing (**JACKIE GLEASON, JACKIE MASON, ART CARNEY, JOHN BALUSHI, PAUL LYND**— et al), big bad Bill will fly into a drunken rage, start a fight, break up the joint and get arrested! After which he'll change his name from "big bad Bill" to "sweet William, now."

VAL KILMER, the one time "Batman" heart-throb is packing on so much beef that his next starring role's gonna be called "Fatman!" Serious physical problems occur following cocaine use in a desperate bid to quickly shed poundage which, ipso facto (ipso *fatso!*), further impairs his health – resulting in cardiac arrest! Only quick action saves his life – possibly the Heimlick Manoeuvre! This he survives and lives to star in more leading roles. (Or should that be *rolls?*)

BEN E. KING, legendary Rhythm & Blues singer and composer of now perennial favorite, ***Stand By Me,*** to be honored with Lifetime Achievement Award. I *see* a multi-colored ribbon and medallion hanging from his neck.

JACQUELINE STALLONE, famed astrologer and mother of superstar actor Sylvester, makes international headlines and becomes the darling of European aristocracy through her accurate planetary prognostications.
SYLVESTER STALLONE must guard health, particularly his overloaded nervous system because the coming year will see him moving ahead by leaps and bounds: producing, acting, writing, real estate, romance (a redhead!) and... the Diplomatic Service?!

Pantomimist great **MARCEL MARCEAU** distinguishes himself by dying *magnificently!* Great honors are bestowed.

Philanthropic Swedish actress **LIV ULLMANN** (Ingmar Bergan's *Face To Face*) takes center stage as she receives honors, accolades and applause for her good works in the field of humanism, especially with children.

LATOYA JACKSON (Micheal's sister) suffers life threatening illness, not unlike those which claimed the life of her one-time husband, the late **JACK GORDON.**

After years of battling tragedy, depression and booze **MARY TYLER MORE,** best known for "wifely" role on the 1960's TV hit series, ***The Dick Van Dyke Show,*** makes a splendiferous but temporary comeback.

PHYLLIS DILLER shocks the (geriatric) world when her new one-woman-show is made into — not only a TV movie but also a movie that younger people will flock to theaters to see. It proves she can still make us laugh, and then she will *pass*.

JACQUELINE STALLONE spins a best-seller detailing her son's success in Hollywood. The talk-show circuit beckons. Deep and *very* dark secrets are revealed.

DICK CLARK'S demise! Scientists examine the 1950's American Bandstand star's brain to try to answer the eternal question: "How the hell did he look so young so long?" Wouldn't ya like to know?

WHITNEY HOUSTON survives latest crisis! Returning to her religious roots, the born again Christian finds the peace and love she desperately seeks. What she feels for **BOBBY BROWN** *IS* real. Roles are reversed when he becomes the caregiver, a loving hus*band* seeking the best specialists in the world for his wife, in order to save her life — but...!

ANGELINA JOLIE and **BRAD PITT** split up, come back and actually stay together awhile, especially since they now have a baby. ("... Everybody loves a baby that's why *I'm* in love with you..., pretty baby, oh-h-h, pretty baby" etc....)

LARRY KING, CNN talk-show giant *may be* dethroned by phenomenally popular **NANCY GRACE** who has risen to the heights through her candor and kindness. Old **LARRY** *could be* put out to pasture now that he's become grumpy, not au current and is content to rest on his laurels.

HOTEL HEIRESS PARIS HILTON'S debut album sells like hot cakes (that is, if you happen to like hot cakes), but all the money in the world can't buy the talent she lacks. **PARIS** should concentrate on her now infamous use of the word "HOT" to launch her "career," as so many other one-hit-wonders have done: For instance, **GOOD TIMES** star **JIMMY (JJ) WALKER** when he commanded a fortune just for coining one word: "**DYN-O-MITE.**" Listen!—there is less to this girl than meets the eye!

* Zinger! O.J. **SIMPSON** makes a temporary comeback, much to the disgust of the **BROWN / GOLDMAN** families of slain ex-wife **NICOLE SIMPSON** and **RONALD GOLDMAN.** Mocking the slayings puts him back in the spotlight! Although disgusting, anything goes nowadays on these **REALITY TV** shows, no matter how offensive! Therefore it is certain to capture the macabre-seeking audience. (* To wit: O.J. offered $5,000,000 for book deal of "If I Did It" version of the case, then cancelled.)

OPRAH'S latest secret surgery, Lap-Band, one of many surgeries she's had—backfires! She falls into a deep depression as a result of interminably seeking perfection and simultaneously slipping into menopause. (Is that a "pause between men?") This has driven and will continue to drive her to seek eternal youth, since she's obviously not quite ready for the "old rockin chair blues." Eventually it's off to the funny farm for the fat frau!

ELIZABETH TAYLOR, making her first public appearance since *The Tonight Show* with the late **JOHNNY CARSON,** denies her latest alleged health problems— including rumors of Alzheimer's. "It's all a publicity stunt!"—she claims. This to maintain her status as Hollywood's queen, since she has little else. It's a desperate plea for attention to keep her place as "the brightest star in the firmament." Stay tuned for more bizarre antics!

ROBERT BLAKE thought he'd bought his way to freedom. He did—but at a price he wasn't expecting to pay, and certain that his old buddies would rally round him, but they did not. ("Shocker!") They've all disappeared. He is friendless and desperately lonely. However, this "little rascal" *will* rebound financially, unlike O.J. "The Juice" Simpson, who will end up...down.

CHRIS ANGEL, star of A&E's hit series *Mind Freak,* finds himself in legal trouble when he pushes the boundaries too far and seriously or fatally injures a spectator participant.

JOHNNY DEPP plays idol KEITH RICHARDS on the big screen—and takes home Oscar for portraying this most colorful member of the Rolling Stones.

SYLVESTER STALLONE achieves superstardom once again with the new *Rambo* flick. Film-goers flock to theaters in record numbers, making him rock!
Baby-boomers continue to love him as they grow old with the characters of *Rocky* & *Rambo*. (Sounds like a pair of cartoon characters: Rocky & Bulwinkle.)

NICOLE RICHIE'S weight loss consumes her life (literally) from drastic measures she employs to stay thin, including a return to her old destructive habits. Girl:—BEWARE!

Iconic singer/actress BARBRA STREISAND, Star of *Her Face Broke Two Mirrors* and now senior citizen, loses her superstar status by pulling yet another spectacular tantrum in front of young cast members in an up-coming special in her honor. (Human—oh, all *too* human!) However JOHN TRAVOLTA'S fat, frumpy impression of this grande dame of song and film in *Hairspray*, will shore up her reputation.

PRINCE CHARLES explodes when **CAMILLA** upstages him publicly and *indecently!* (Surprise, surprise!) Embarrassing the Royal Family once again, this time **QUEEN ELIZABETH** freezes her out for good. (… At least until Her Majesty passes into the Great Beyond!)

HILLARY CLINTON proves she still loves ex- Pres. hubby BILL, by running for the office of U.S. President and declaring "Sweet William" her personal secretary. ("Well!…ah d-o-o de-cla-a-a-re!" "Well *ah* don't, and that's how I get to keep it all!")

MARTHA STEWART'S popularity temporarily slides when rumors of another investment scam leak out. Still, she remains as popular as ever.

Infamous **DON INUS** (hey—it rhymes!) of the world-class faux pas: "nappy-headed ho-" crack, survives all this—and more!—even brutal cutting remarks from **HOWARD** the "Shock Jock" king himself, and rises to super-stardom, deposing old eagle beak **STERN** in the process.

PHIL SPECTOR accidentally shoots himself in the face (if you can call *that* a face) as he demonstrates how she did indeed shoot herself likewise. The entire scene is replete with **LAUREL & HARDY / ABBOTT & COSTELLO** comic relief. (Sheesh—what a schlemiel! Or should that be schlemozzle.) The defense argues that it's too far-fetched *not* to be true.

WHOOPIE GOLDBERG makes such outrageous statements on *The View* that fans are left panting for more! (And you can't go through life in short pants! —Nyuk, nyuk.)
    With no-holds barred rhetoric, *Snoopy* (Whoopie) finally breaks through the "strict" guidelines of the current, dull and monotonous goody-two-shoes dialogue to make this the hottest show in America!

Onetime superstar **MICHEAL JACKSON** attempts suicide in a vain effort to join his beloved career, which is also dead…. But alas, here too he fails. Oh, les miserable!

He's cutting off his nose to spite his face—oh, sorry, I forgot—he's already done that.

The music industry—"dancing as fast as it can" to turn out new flash-in-the-pan groups and singers and hoping to find *real* talent—resorts once again to the glorious past and those "Golden Oldies," rerecording those great tunes that time cannot tarnish... Ahh, yes:... "Those were the days, my friend, I thought they'd *never* end...," etc (but they did, didn't they?)

Popular **JUDGE JUDY** finds herself in big legal trouble when they discover her tax returns are fudged. It gives her multi-million dollar TV series a whole new meaning perhaps: "Law & Hoarder?"

WOODY ALLEN, ever fearful of dying (who isn't?) finally has to face the "grim reaper" when he succumbs to a heart attack! However not before enjoying an incredible run of great good luck and even more success. Everybody's favorite neurotic always says: "I don't mind dying, I just don't wanna be there when it happens!" And he won't, it'll be *that* quick!

ELIZABETHB TAYLOR, as her mind continues "to wander," leaves a large chunk of change to another **LARRY FORTENSKY**-type, much to the chagrin of family and friends. However, he proves to be a good butler / assistant / caregiver as was the late "large mouthed" **MARTHA RAY'S** "companion." But one day Liz will awake to "wonder where the butler went," when she goes to the bank and finds "her money spent!"

"Old snake eyes" **JACK NICOLSON** accepts roles to match *his* own (stomach rolls) that are more suited to *Grumpy Old Men* characters. As age and weight take their toll, turning Jake into a laughable, but no so lovable character and forcing him to step—uh, I mean—*waddle*, out of the rough, tough, romantic hero leads, he truly will become the "One Who Flew Over The Cuckoo's Nest" as he slips further into old age senility, *without* the lobotomy.

Illusionist **CHRIS ANGEL** shall die by his own hand as one "trick pony" too many goes wrong. After injuring one spectator, another shall end in flaming morte! Within one, two or three, shall it *be*!

BOUNTY HUNTER DWAYNE "DOG" CHAPMAN, suffering a terrible nervous breakdown because of financial and legal woes, goes berserk and ends up back in the BIG HOUSE (or the nut house).

Reality TV is becoming to *unreal* for the public and will be replaced by *real* life reality shows! (If that makes any sense to you.) Networks will "buy" *ordinary* lives of everyday people: —suicides, wife beatings, etc. — which prove to be more entertaining than the rehearsed "reality" versions.

STAR JONES abandons her new TV show because of health problems. She can't do it alone but may survive with a good partner sharing the load.

BRITNEY SPEARS temporarily loses custody of her children, and she needs to shock her back to reality for her own sake and her children's.

BRAD PITT—feeling rather smothered by his *"bitter"* half, **ANGELINA JOLIE**—wants out! It's not worth the power struggle to stay together for appearances sake. Brad is searching for his soul mate, but he may have already found her in actor **JOHN VOIGHT'S** daughter, but doesn't realize it.

ZSA ZSA GABOR, socialite actress and former *Moulin Rouge* star (1953) pens a "tell all" book naming names and revealing some of Hollywood's best-kept secrets, possibly ruining a few good careers in the process. Those whom she feels have abandoned her.

AL PACINO and **ROBERT DeNIRO** come to blows in a public place over who is the tougher of the two! That's Hollywood movie tough, of course. It'll look more like a **HAL ROACH** comedy than a real fist fight, since neither one couldn't fight his way out of a wet paper bag, as the saying goes.

KIRK RUSSELL and long time squeeze **GOLDIE HAWN** will team to produce a smash box office hit that breaths new life into Tinseltown, their careers and even finds its way to *Broadway* (a reversal of the usual procedure).

Freshly divorced **EDDIE MURPHY** reeks havoc on Tinseltown (again?) by using it to pursue drag racing and *drag queens!*

DONALD TRUMP remains true to form when first ex-wife **IVANA** remarries, irking him to shoot off his mouth again, but this time leaving the egg on *his* face.... Nice "irk" if you can get it.

Unctuous **ERIC ROBERTS,** infamous brother of Julia, suffers another tragic motorcycle accident that leaves him crippled!—like his career!

Bourne Ultimatum star **MATT DAMON** becomes the new number one action hero, leaving poor **TOM CRUISE** awa-a-a-ay out in the cold along with his attempt to rise back up as top dog—which is to say it's pretty much a "mission impossible."

LIZA MINELLI astounds everyone with her resilient star power by producing, directing and starring in a hugely successful *Broadway* play that in part mocks ex-hubby **CHRISTOPHER GUEST** and their brief (and bizarre) relationship.

Ex-football star **MICHAEL VICKS**, because of his cruelty to animals, will *never* again set foot on a sports field or be asked to promote product brand names. He is in a word—finished, done (like dinner)—tout fini!

NICOLE RITCHIE gives birth only to have "empty arms" when the baby is removed from her "loving" care. Hospital tests reveal suspicious drugs.

HULK HOGAN—"Mr. Wrestling"—comes out publicly against steroid use as he himself slowly disintegrates from his own former use of the drug.

BILL ("SWEET WILLIAM") COSBY shocks fans when tabloids reveal he *may* have been deeply involved with the notorious BLACK PANTHER movement. You shall hear, in this way or that, new startling revelations of his sons tragic death.

PAUL McCARTNEY surprises the world by marrying a more suitable and better grounded HEATHER LOCKLEAR, America's long time sweetheart.

O.J.'S book opens a can of worms and a new investigation into the two horrific murders, possibly sending lawyers to jail because of evidence withheld from trial.... Nonetheless in the "court of public opinion" he is still—and always shall be—incredibly guilty!

Tragedy for ROD STEWART as his troubled son, Sean, accidentally overdoses!

OPRAH becomes opposed to plastic surgery, serving as a role model for young black women everywhere.

DICK CLARK makes a temporary recovery but backslides into ill health, rendering the beloved 50's "American Bandstand" icon a recluse until his death.

PHYLLIS DILLER performs yet one more time before joining that "great gag gang" in the sky.

BRAD PITT'S world is rocked when ANGELINA returns briefly to her gay lover before finding herself "pregers" again. But by whom?!

TORI SPELLING's grief over daddy's death lessens considerably when the cheque arrives.

ASHLEE SIMPSON, over-shadowed by big sis JESSICA, once again ends up on a collision course with drugs and booze.

PRESIDENT BUSH hides the fact that he and wife **LAURA** have been living separately for years!

Gay marriage to be re-vamped as "same sex marriage," but not without a lot of boo-hooing.

NICOLE KIDMAN pens a book about bizarre marriage to **SCIENTOLOGY** adherent **TOM CRUISE**. It'll expose the outrageous co-habitations of the rich, (weird) and infamous!

LIZ TAYLOR'S bizarre antics, possibly the effects of Alzheimer's (or Part-Timer's) disease, starts Hollywood tongues wagging when she begins wandering around old haunts of bygone years, attempting to recapture her glory days by re-enacting, in public, for all to witness, some of her more famous (and infamous) roles. But none (– *the antics!* –) will be so bizarre as that which is coming round the bend – and coming fast!

JULIA ROBERTS is flabbergasted when yet again twins arrive!

JERRY SPRINGER will pass the baton to his right-hand man, **STEVE,** when he retires at age 64 (two years hence) to run for Governor of Ohio.

GENE SIMMONS, former **KISS** star, loses his reality show to the rest of the family when the audience requests more air time for his beauty queen wife, former *Playboy* cover girl **SHANNON TWEED.** This re-ignites *her* career!

FIDEL CASTRO "retires" and allow his brother to take the reins. Slowly, the grip of Communism in Cuba loosens and mercifully the old warrior will not live to see his years of tireless ruling go down the drain.

PAUL McCARTNEY "brushes" with death when his electric tooth-brush, in proximity to the water on the tile floor where he stands barefoot, is not properly grounded and he's zapped! Actually he gets the *brush* twice — the first time from his ex.

RICHARD REMAROUS, aka the **NIGHT STALKER,** attempts suicide but is saved in the "nick" of time, said nick being the carotid artery!

SCOTT PETERSON, who murdered his pregnant wife **LACEY PETERSON**, wins an appeal when new evidence comes to light. **AMBER FREY,** his then girlfriend, admits (after a severe attack of conscience) that she was *much more involved* than people had originally thought.

PRINCE CHARLES'S wife, **CAMILLA PARKER BOWLES,** blows the lid off their marriage by offering up incriminating and damaging evidence to the press about her husband's and mother-in-law **QUEEN ELIZABETH'S** involvement in the death of **PRINCESS DIANA!** Murder most foul!

OPRAH is sideswiped when ex-beau **STEADMAN** de-idolizes her spotless reputation by revealing her not-so-secret gay life with gal pal, **GAIL.**

GEORGE BUSH faints in front of "all the President's men" in the Oval Office after suffering a severe anxiety attack, leaving them to assume he croaked! Lying there (as well as lying there) he hears horrible comments about him as he plays possum and listens to their disposal plans—of him!

HEATHER LOCKLEAR dates only top Hollywood executives! She's more than paid her dues and holds the record for "staying power." This (new) "most sexy leading lady" will star in a role so suited to her style that she'll finally win the praise so long due her.

BRUCE WILLIS surrenders and accepts elderly-type roles because he has no choice but to hang up his action cape for the rocking-chair-wisdom of the printed word! Well, he's got to make a buck somehow! But remember: "the (action of the) pen is mightier than the sword." **JACK NICHOLSON** becomes the new **MARLON BRANDO** as strange and bizarre behavior renders him (even more) eccentric and reclusive, leaving Hollywood no choice but to cater to his every crazy whim as he actually *becomes* the character he portrayed in *As Good As It Gets*. (A clear case of life imitating art.)

WOODY ALLEN surprises everyone by finally setting foot outside his beloved New York to do a film in California. Doom and gloom Allen breaks out in a rash and simply cannot create anywhere other than back in "his own home town," where he'll turn out yet another black-and-white masterpiece.

Oscars soon enough for fine performances turned in by **EDWARD NORTON** (no, not **JACKIE GLEASON's ED NORTON**) and **PAUL GIAMATTI,** boths fine actors.

ADRIEN BRODY won a Oscar for his stunning performance in *The Pianist*. But as a romantic lead and tough guy private eye in follow up films such as *King Kong* and *Hollywoodland* respectively, he is woefully lacking in that he was terribly miscast. A remake of Cyrano deBergerac would have served him better. I "see" a nose job in his future. Right now he looks like a tired anteater.

Canadian Showbiz:

KEIFFER SUTHERLAND forsakes acting for politics to follow in the footsteps of his revered grandfather, **TOMMY DOUGLAS,** who created Canada's Health system that's available to rich and *poor* alike. Vouch safing it for the next generation, Mr. Sutherland (the junior) becomes a hero, humanitarian and perhaps the Prime Minister of Canada.

BOB BARKER *(The Price is Right)* passes peacefully while doing what he loves best – golf? womanizing? drinking? – "cutting up jackpots" with his carny friends?... But you can "bet your life" that when the game show icon is called up yonder, he'll certainly importune the BIG GUY to first "let's make a deal!"

Some day Native Canadian **ADAM BEACH** will win a special Oscar for his good works on behalf of all North American Natives.

Fire from the sky devastates Fairmont Chateau Lake Louise and Banff Springs hotels—simultaneously! A natural, widespread catastrophe—perhaps a great meteor or a Krakatoa-like explosion! (...Or maybe just "Jewish lightning?")

NEW MAPLE LEAF SPORTS AND ENTERTAINMENT CENTRE in Toronto, Canada—collapses like a house of cards! Miraculously no one is hurt. To quote the usual police statement to the press: "...foul play is suspected, round up the usual suspects."

Canada's **"STOMPIN' " TOM CONNORS** goes to Hollywood?!

Canadian Rock & Roll legend **"ROMPIN" RONNIE HAWKINS,** virtually returned from the *dead*, heads up hot new band to star in TV variety series.

Former **CANDIAN PRIME MINISTER BRIAN MULRONY** succumbs! The shock causes his son, **BEN MULRONY** (journalist and television personality), serious injury in an auto mishap. (P.S.—Shouldn't ride in helicopters, either.)

Vancouver, B.C. crooner **MICHAEL BUBLE** suffers serious throat problems that curtail his burgeoning career. Probably polyps. Do not despair, "bubbly" boy, an acting career beckons with open arms, —and the open arms of a new love.

"Black still in the Red!" I prophesied long ago, when **LORD CON-RAD of CROSSHARBOUR** was still a mere Canadian: "**CONRAD BLACK** will rue the day he gave up his birthright, his citizenship, to become a peer of the realm. A scandal will send him scurrying home with his tail between his legs!"… The man will be stripped of every-thing, what with business and legal woes.

BLACK retains **EDWARD GREENSPAN**: "A law for the rich and a law for the poor," they say. However in this *case* (no pun intended) justice truly is blind, and when Canadian defense lawyer **EDWARD (EDDY) GREENSPAN** is retained, also deaf and dumb! It's the kiss of death for some of his clients. Of the several high profile Canadian defendants he has acted for (convicted murderers Demeter, Buxbaum, etc), not only have they gone to jail for life—which, by the way, is a big joke in Canada—they've also had to pay good old Eddy about a million bucks in fees! (The unkindest cut of all!) Lucky for them there's no death penalty in Canada—yet. Mores the pity.

In my predictions over the many long years, I have *emphasized* that Canada must and *will* build its armed forces to the point in which it once took pride during World Wars I and II, when it became the third most powerful army in the world! Not only to protect our shores from sneak attacks from so-called "terrorists" (—and to my mind they are nothing more than snakes with arms and legs, terrorist being too generous an appellation for them), but also for protection from within. The armies of all Western Countries shall let loose the dogs of war from *within* its own borders to weed out the vermin!

Believe it or not! The Canadian Government takes a referendum to the people on the death penalty—which passes!

CANADIAN PRIME MINISTER, STEPHEN HARPER, *will* win three terms before stepping down for health (and injury) reasons. In-jury from putting himself in the direct line of fire! He will not see the end of his third term….

As restitution is made to Canadian Chinese citizens or their descen-dants for the degrading Head Tax put on them to enter Canada, so too will all Native peoples (Canadian Natives) come into their own as they nationally unite. One loud and powerful voice in Ottawa.

CURTIS SILVA'S world famous Guardian Angels continue to grow and prosper as they prove themselves an important adjustment to the general protection of society. If Toronto's Mayor Miller wants to win office again, *I strongly urge* he "get on side." (P.S. — Mr. Miller: keep fighting against the building of a bridge to the Island, because if you lose *that one* you might as well give up the ghost altogether!)

Tenor singer **JOHN McDERMOTT** makes international headlines and is awarded the Medal of Valor! Perhaps for entertaining Canadian troops abroad? Or simply for entertaining a broad?... (Who happens to be *very* ugly?)

Whoever is responsible for the destruction of the venerable Toronto landmark generally known as "The Inn On Park," be they one or twenty-one, shall suffer eternal economic damnation as will any edifice erected on that site, thereafter and forever.

(As so tragically demonstrated by the demise of the hundred-year-old Toronto Lowe's Uptown Theatre, by a young man's death from a crashing wall! Buildings have souls, too....)

Medicine/ Science: Around the World

To the delight of former actor and current Parkinson's sufferer **MICHAEL J. FOX,** a new wonder drug shows such great promise that it exceeds even *his* expectations when testing moves from animal to human and eliminates symptoms entirely; ipso facto, a cure!

Medical science quickly discovers antidotes for most chemicals with which al-Qaida threatens the West, rendering them (the chemicals) harmless, because civilians and solders alike will be inoculated.

The increase of people text messaging on cell phones creates a new kind of carpal tunnel syndrome that baffles doctors.

A new steroid is being developed that is virtually undetectable by today's tests. It's hoped it will create an unstoppable Olympic Team.

A humongous squid from the ocean depths washes up somewhere on the coast of B.C. (British Columbia) or Washington State. As long as a football field, nothing quite like it has ever been seen before. – And still alive!

Children born of drug dependent parents shall at long last escape "the sins of the father" through an incredible gene manipulation breakthrough. The procedure, made possible through the mapping of the entire genome system, allows for the exact pinpointing of the "addictive" gene, thus neutralizing its effects and forever removing this curse that shall no longer determine the destinies of our children.

Every year, younger and younger men and women are spending big bucks on various plastic surgeries in search of that elusive "fountain of youth." Soon to reach pathological proportions (such as anorexia nervosa and bulimia currently have), this entire generation will forsake *that* "fountain" to begin searching for another: – the "pot of gold at the end of the rainbow" – so broke will they be from shelling out *their plastic* to the plastic surgeons.

A gemstone radiating a strange healing power through its ambient light is NOT-OF-THIS-WORLD!

In a South American rain forest, the bark of a rare *rope tree* is found to cure arthritis.

As in **H.G. WELLS'** *Time Machine*, a subterranean culture evolves as our sun gradually loses power and the Earth its ozone layer. Whole peoples literally will come *out of the ground* like night-crawlers!

Humankind will breed itself out of its current state to metamorphose into an efficient, more sophisticated animal, where important decisions are less dependent on emotion and more on cerebral content. (Not quite like the Nazis, though – they were a little *too* efficient!)

Illegal steroids become legit, as did the numbers racket and bootlegging (now beer and liquor stores) before them. But they, too, like the above mentioned government-run "businesses," *should be used* in moderation.

Only society's elite, the plutocrats (the very wealthy) will journey to the outer planets beyond our solar system for surgical procedures; the technology of which does not yet exist on Earth is being kept from us; technology that is extraterrestrial in nature. "...And the meek (which rhymes with *weak*) shall inherit the Earth." [CHRISTIAN BIBLE]

The expression "computer friendly" shall exeunt stage left when doctors and scientist discover over use is causing all kinds of eye problems – even permanent blindness! (SIT WELL BACK FROM THE SCREEN!!!)

As I have prophesied: continuous cell phone use *will* result in serious brain damage to our children's children. "...And the sins of the father shall visit upon the children." [CHRISTIAN BIBLE]

We have fished the oceans dry and restocked them with genetically altered ikhthus (fish). The consequences will be staggering.... In the coming years, decades and centuries, denizens of the deep that consume these "fish" will grow into *real* – not imagined chimeric monsters – but real GIANT squids, sharks, eels – even the ancient prehistoric ichthyosaur (heavens to betsy! – shades of old Nessie, the Loch Ness Monster!) that can function on land as well as in water. Pre-Jurassic age doth return!

Outer space moves closer as shuttles oscillate between Earth and permanent space stations. But some day thousands will

travel to these suspended "platforms" by means of a super elevator, like a great Silver thread from the Earth, even to the
moon – and beyond!

Simple home visits from doctors take up to two weeks as national medical systems begin to fail. However, quick steps taken
– save *all*!

I have prophesied for years: America *will* adopt one of the national systems for its very own, for a country is only as strong as
its weakest and most helpless citizen. Soon, a very wise and
powerful American will bring this obvious fact to the attention
of Congress – with success!

Selective amnesia becomes medical fact instead of a joke when
scientists discover a "functioning" gene (for want of a better
word) in the elderly that *naturally* suppresses unpleasant memories (in most cases) while preserving pleasant ones. It acts as a
kind of self-defense mechanism. Psychiatrists will give it a new
appellation in order to cash in.

(To Pass…)

NOAH CHOMSKY, American theoretical linguist, noted for his
theory of generative grammar and for demonstrating that *all* lan-
guages share the same underlying grammatical base, will be shot
to death by a foreign mugger because he (the thief) could not
communicate to him that all he wanted was his wallet. "What we
have here, is failure to *communicate*." *(Cool Hand Luke)*

A mighty transformational method of treating heart attack vic-
tims as well as those with congestive heart failure is on the very
threshold of discovery! Patients who would be doomed to an
invalid's existence, followed by a slow, suffocating and agonizing death will suddenly receive a new lease on life, thanks to
the discovery of a gene cell whose implantation or injection immediately repairs damaged vessels and arteries! (…Something
like liquid car radiator repair.)

Grow new breasts? Emotionally traumatized women who have survived single and double mastectomies will be able to regrow—like a second set of teeth—their mammary glands, thanks to an extraordinary scientific breakthrough in cellular regeneration and cloning. (It'll also be good for broads who had no tits to start with!) Implants become a thing of the past as women keep *abreast* of the situation. (Nyuck, nyuck.)

The blind will see! Incredible breakthrough in the discovery of and transplantation from heretofore unknown "sight centers" in the brain. Not only will it benefit the visually-impaired, but people who have been totally blind since birth will actually see — see the natural beauty of this planet wrought by nature (and hopefully not its ugliness wrought by man).

DR. JAY CHAPMAN, who concocted the triple-header cocktail used in lethal injections in prisons throughout America, will himself *pass* in like manner, either by his own hand or by a "state-sanctioned" executioner. (Possibly for murder!) Similar to Dr. Guillotine (1738-1814) who, after inventing the contraption that quickly "sliced and diced," was himself sliced and diced!

Organ donations by the living — for pay — is the next big thing! Indigent people will see this as the new lottery — a "get rich quick!" scheme. Kidneys, corneas and liver (parts) will go for a million (U.S) and put him or her on easy street. Some may be so dumb as to try to sell their hearts for transplants, not realizing the somewhat slightly fatal consequence. Not fatal to lawyers, though. They could never *miss* that which was never there to begin with!

My slogan, **"Dead Legs Will Walk Again,"** takes yet another *giant leap* nearer its goal as scientists come closer to repairing the entire neurological system due to damage through disease or injury. Ditto for glaucoma, MS (Multiple Sclerosis) and MD

(Muscular Dystrophy) and all the other alphabet soup diseases!

Artificial sweeteners used in colas and various beverages will be taken off the market because of links to **cancer.**

We will see the establishment of human euthanasia centers as the mass of infirmed humanity becomes overwhelming.

Life gets easier for the elderly when allowed to vote for medications *they* deem important.

DNA is the key to *all* life…. People won't be able to reproduce unless their "juice" is tested.

New Age discovery reveals swimming is the new "fountain of youth" eagerly sought after by aging baby-boomers.

Research reveals that animal companions for the elderly prove to be valuable in the treatment of Alzheimer's. People relate better to dogs and cats than to humans because of their soothing effect. (Unless of course it happens to be a pissed-off Pit Bull!)

It's discovered that fruit and their extracts — especially strawberries and blueberries — is the answer to many cancer cure variations. Articles in Medical Journals abound!

The elderly become crucial for survival studies. Young medical professionals learn the DNA path to longevity.

A new line of clothing becomes the new "It!" Wearing biodegradable materials is gonna be the next big thing to hit Tinsletown. Just watch!

Music plays an important role in the treatment of many diseases as new techniques are sought after to help speed recovery time, especially for the elderly.

A miracle cure for Rheumatoid Arthritis is accidently stumbled upon. Like most useful discoveries, it surprises the scientists!

A trend emerges involving farm animal tissue injections that proves to be a money-making hoax. (And a great failure, except for the guy *making* the millions!)

People sixty and over cease seeking the plastic surgery remedy for that youthful look. Instead, aging naturally, with knowledge of good old-fashioned nutrition and love becomes the new norm—even in Hollywood!

Seniors flock to theaters to enjoy films that reflects more serious aspects of life. Movie houses will slowly die because of overpaid, no talent actors. Unknown personalities will light up the screen and breath new life into the old flickrs.

Earth continues to wither from products of the "new economy," but a great person—to whom all listen— gives up the secret to eternal life! In hushed silence everyone waits for the answer, and the answer is: ..."What was the question?"

"Inner strength," character and integrity are the qualites for which young people are searching. Cultivating these qualities will help to ensure a *chance* at health, happiness and love. *"Spiritual strength,"* whatever works for you, will carry the day.

Pandemic disease wipes out Mankind! "Unaffected" survivors become progenitors of a new breed who respect simple things: clean air, green foliage…trees, cool weather.…

Scorching heat drives the peoples of this world underground, rendering a species of human-like aliens!

It's discovered that "altered mental states" (including schizophrenia) are the result of *finely-tuned, ultra-sensitive* Electrical impulses interacting "badly" with <u>E</u>lectrical particles or Electrical waves of other people and of the <u>U</u>niverse, which are then carried to and fro through the Ether — the Ether which is *also* <u>E</u>lectrically charged and is both a transmitter and reciever.

Treatment and control will be a mild alternating current, much like a pacemaker. This current can be triggered by any unusual or aberrant power spike anywhere in the brain, rendering the patient reasonable and content. In short, it is the return of 1930's Electric Shock Therapy — sneaking in through the back door! Schizophrenia will be all but eradicated! ESP becomes the new science, sans religion and superstition, and is placed in the realm of physics, where it belongs!

Severed or amputated limbs grow back! Even on people born without, through the re-discovery of the amphibian gene.

Sports:

The St. Louis Cardinals win the World Series!

GRETSKY'S team turn heads when they start winning game after game – but turn stomachs during the finals after a disgusting display of sportsmanship costs them four consecutive games. I see "the Great One" in a great despair!

TIGER WOODS, noted for long drives, is publicly humiliated when steel balls, cleverly disguised in his driver to ensure extra power, are uncovered. (Or should that be steel balls discovered, one on each side of his *driver*.) Following this, the only *long drives* he'll make will be in his car – to the countryside, trying to escape the embarrassment.

TIGER WOODS, attempting a comeback from the above mentioned scandal, can't quite cut it. His fickle fans begin referring to him as "*kitty*" and "*pussy*" Woods, instead of Tiger.

When super soccer player **DAVID BECKHAM** returns to "the colonies" to *promote* soccer, the *reverse* occurs and North Americans turn away from the pretty boy from Limey-land because of his public shenanigans.

BECKHAM has a punch-up in one of Tinseltown's better known eateries. Although his body is broken and bruised, his ego is more so. To add insult to injury, he also ends up with food poisoning! (Some days ya' just can't win.)

When **BECKHAM** bites off more than he can chew, he finally blows his top! Both his family and career suffer badly for it.

MAGIC JOHNSON, basketball great and HIV sufferer, emerges from seclusion to host one of America's most popular TV shows.

MICHAEL JORDAN, another former basketball great, produces and stars in an autobiographical movie, focusing first on his father's life and death.

"**TIGER WOODS** suffers major stroke on golf course after powerful drive!" This puts (that's puts—not putts) him out of commission for good, never to regain his status as NO. 1. But a valiant effort, nonetheless.

NOSTRADAMUS

From the Complete Prophecies of Nostradamus. By Henry C. Roberts: First published 1947, last published 1975.
*Note: Any references to the "New-World" or the "New City" refers to "America," since most of his prophecies were made circa 1555 — shortly after Christopher Columbus discovered the New World— America! (Anthony Carr)

New York twin towers catastrophe!!!
Quatrain 97, p. 211: "The heaven shall burn at five and forty degrees. The fire shall come near the great 'New City!' In an instant a great flame dispersed shall burst out, when they shall make a trail of the Normans."
Interpretation: "A cataclysmic fire shall engulf the greatest and 'newest' of the world's big cities." New York City is exactly forty-five degrees latitude! — plus, both planes hit the buildings at approximately 45 degrees latitude! (Anthony Carr)

The attack on New York City:
Quatrain 87, p. 37: "Ennosige, fire of the center of the earth, Shall make an earthquake of the New City, Two great rocks (World Trade Centers?) shall long time war against each other, after that, Arethusa shall colour red the fresh river."
Interpretation: "A terrific fire, of the same nature as that at the center of the earth, shall make a shambles of the 'New (York?) City.' " Arethusa was an ever flowing classic spring. (Anthony Carr)

The attack on New York City:
Quatrain 190, p. 144: "Fire shall fall from the skies on the King's palace (World Trade Centers?). When Mar's light shall be eclipsed, Great War shall be for seven months, people shall die by witchcraft, Rouen and Eureux shall not fail the King."
Interpretation: "A seven month's war of tremendous destructive force such as the world has never seen before shall terrify mankind!" (Anthony Carr)

Second attack on America:

Quatrain 23, p. 118: "The Legion in the Maritime Fleet, Calcening greatly, shall burn brimstone and pitch, after a long rest in the secure place (America, fifty-seven relatively peaceful years since end of WW II), they shall seek Port Selyn, but fire shall consume them."

Interpretation: "A terrific assault by a great fleet equipped with weapons employing potent chemical agents (Anthrax, etc.) shall attack a country which has long enjoyed peace and security (America). They shall attack the great Port of Les N.Y. but will be repulsed (by America) by weapons even more terrible!" (Anthony Carr)

Attack on America (New York):

Quatrain 72, p. 336: "In the year 1999 and seven months, from the skies shall come an invasion, a 'war of the worlds,' to raise again the powerful and mighty King of Jacquerie (King of the peasants), before and after, Mars (war) shall reign at will!"

Interpretation: "I'm certain this refers to the attack on New York and the Pentagon. Although Nostradamus was off by two years, I stated at the time that this event will occur even though the predicted date has passed. And, we may yet face an invasion from another world...Only time will tell."

"A tremendous world revolution is foretold to take place in the year 1999 (2001), with a complete upheaval of existing social orders, preceded by world-wide wars, followed by an epoch of peace, a Uni-religion and One world leader, who restores and keeps the peace." (Anthony Carr)

Osama bin Laden, the Antichrist, and the Armageddon predictions. Quotes from: Nostradamus: Countdown to Apocalypse, by John Charles de Fontbryne. "Soiled by murders and abominable crimes, this great enemy of the human race will be worse than all his predecessors! By the sword and flame of war he will shed blood in inhuman fashion!" (P.421, CX, Q10)

"The Antichrist will soon annihilate three countries. The war he will wage will last twenty-seven years. Opponents will be put to death and prisoners deported. Blood from bodies will redden the water, the land will be riddled with blows (missiles, bombardments)." (P.423, CVIII, Q17)

"The airborne invasion of New York in July, 1999 (September 11, 2001). A great and terrifying leader will come through the skies to revive (the memory of) the great conqueror Angoulême. Before and after, war will rule luckily." (Cx, 972)
Interpretation: "Obviously, New York City." (Anthony Carr)

Powerful enemy hidden within bosom of New York City. Quatrain 92, p.308: "The King shall desire to enter into the 'New City.' With foes they shall come to overcome it, The prisoner being freed, shall speak and act falsely, The King being gotten out, shall keep far from enemies."
Interpretation: "The 'New City' (New York?) shall be besieged by a powerful person, helped by spies within!" (Anthony Carr)

A tidal wave of putrid water throughout New York, New Jersey or Atlantic City.
Quatrain 49, p. 328: "Garden of the World (Garden State?), near the New City (New York?), in the way of the man-made mountains (Skyscrapers?), shall be seized on and plunged into a ferment (putrid), being forced to drink sulphurous poisoned waters." **Interpretation:** "This startling prophecy of a catastrophic event at a pleasure resort not far from the great 'new city' predicts a tremendous tidal wave of poisoned waters that shall sweep in from 'the resort' and overwhelm the man-made mountain-like skyscrapers of the city." (Anthony Carr)

One religion—for all!
Quatrain 72, p. 302: "Once more shall the Holy Temple be polluted, And deprecated by the Senate of Toulouse; Saturn two, three cycles revolving, In April, May, people of a new heaven."
Interpretation: "According to this prophecy, there will be a complete revision of the basic concepts of religion about the year 2150 (600 years after it was written), and a 'New-World' (America?) Order will arise." (Possibly one religion for all—when the Star-travelers return!). (Anthony Carr)

Terrible war, followed by a 'New-World' leader who will initiate a long peace.
Quatrain 24, p. 187: "Mars and the Secptre, being conjoined together,

Under Cancer shall be a calamitous war, A little while after a new King shall be anointed, who, for a long time, shall pacify the earth."
Interpretation: "Nostradamus here speaks of a constellation called the Sceptre. Looking at what was then the far future (1555), he foretells of a time when this constellation shall be in conjunction with Mars and the terrible war that will break out under this influence. And out of the debacle there will arise a "New-World" leader ("New-World," United States President?) and peace will reign for a long time afterward." (Anthony Carr)

Quatrain 70, p. 202: "A chief of the world, the great Henry shall be, at first, beloved, afterwards feared, dreaded, his fame and praise shall go beyond the heavens! And shall be contented with the title of Victor."
Interpretation: "The nations will organize a super-government covering the entire world! The president will be called, or named, Henry. 'Chryen' by transposition of letters is an anagram for 'Henry,' then current form of Henry." (Anthony Carr)

Eventual world peace (egalitarianism)
Quatrain 10, p. 182: "Within a little while the temples of the colors, white and black shall be intermixed, red and yellow shall take away their colors; blood, earth, plague, famine, fire, water shall destroy them."
Interpretation: "After a period of much travail all the races of the world shall lose their prejudices and be as one." (Anthony Carr)
Quatrain 89, pg. 341: "The walls shall be turned from brick into marble, There shall be peace for seven and fifty years, Joy to mankind; the aqueduct shall be rebuilt, health, abundance of fruits, joys and a mellifluous time."
Interpretation: "Nostradamus predicts a golden age for humanity after a great calamitous war among nations. *Personally, I think this refers to the end of World War II 'till the present — exactly fifty seven years (1945-2002), then hostilities begin anew!" (Anthony Carr)

Yet another prediction of eventual world peace.
Quatrain 66, p. 300: "Peace, union, shall be and profound changes, estates, offices, the low high and the high very low. A journey shall be prepared for, the first fruit, pains, war shall cease, also civil processes and strife."

Interpretation: "A Utopian age shall come into being in the course of time, but not without pain."

Quatrain 96, p. 344: "Religion of the name of the seas shall come against the Sect of 'Caitif of the Moon.' The deplorably obstinate sect shall be afraid of the two wounded by A. and A." Interpretation: "One must delve deeply into these cryptic words in order to grasp their full meaning. The 'Caitifs of the Moon' indicates the Arab nation. The phrase "A. and A." means America. The sense, then, is that there will be a struggle between the opposing philosophies of the two groups." (*To say the least!)

Now we can see it: "Religion of the name of the seas shall come against the 'Sect of Caitifs of the Moon.' (Arab Nations' flag is the quarter-moon and star; the word 'Caitif,' in the Unabridged Oxford Dictionary means: "base, cowardly and despicable"); the deplorably obstinate sect shall be afraid of the two wounded by A. and A. The sneaky, cowardly murderous fanatics shall become afraid of, then destroyed by, A. and A. —America!!! (Anthony Carr)

The sudden end of global war!

Quatrain 53, p. 162: "The law of Sun and Venus contending, appropriating the spirit of prophecy, neither one nor the other shall be heard. By Sol the law of the great Messiah shall subsist."

Interpretation: "The forces of light and darkness, struggling for domination over the spirit of man, shall both be superseded by the new law of the great Savior!" (*Or, if I may suggest, The Great and Mighty One will halt the carnage, "lest all flesh perish!"... The Supreme Star-traveler, or God, who created us all — Christian, Muslim and Jew.) (Anthony Carr)

Quatrain 99, p. 345: "At last the wolf, the lion, ox and ass, the gentle doe, shall be down with mastiffs. The manna shall no more fall to them, There shall be no more watching and keeping of mastiffs." Interpretation: "This reiterates previous prognostications of a period of peace and plenty, and the elimination of war."

And peace shall come at last!!! (Anthony Carr)

Religion
Was God A Star-Traveler?

Revelation of Anthony Carr:

I remember vividly the dark and windy October night, many years ago, when I received the amazing revelation I am about to relate.

I was sitting by the fireside in my home by the lake. Feeling discontented and restless, I took a book from my large library of mystic and occult literature and began to peruse through it. The volume was called *Religious Iconography of The Ancient World*, written by an obscure nineteenth century academic.

I was studying a picture of a religious artifact representing The Sacred Scarab Beetle, used by the ancient Egyptian priesthood, when suddenly, without warning, the book flew out of my hands and landed at my feet, upside down!

I saw immediately from this angle that the picture of the insect was quite different, it actually portrayed very clearly the image of a gigantic spacecraft landing or leaving in a blaze of fire and smoke! This revelation was the beginning of my lifelong obsession with the idea that The Star-traveler / "Lord of Lords" had visited the earth in ancient time, and his appearance is revealed in the images of pagan literature, as well as the Bible.

The Scarab Beetle has long been regarded as an ancient Egyptian symbol of myth and magic. But is it a beetle?

What would a dung beetle have to do with religion, reverence and mysticism? Perhaps it is not a beetle at all!

For five thousand years we may have been looking at this picture *from the wrong angle.* Turn it upside down and you will see an amazing image, that of a magnificent space craft which is landing (or blasting off) in an explosion of light and flames!

Now we can see why this image, when viewed from the proper perspective, was held in such reverence and high regard by The Ancients!

The mystical, magical Scarab Beetle of Egypt was for thousands of years an object of reverence but people have been looking at it *upside down!*

Not This Way...

Photograph of an ancient Egyptian religious artifact which clearly shows the image of the Sacred Scarab Beetle.

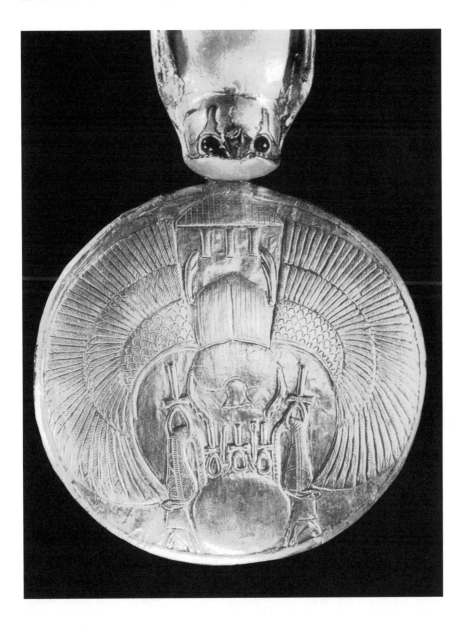

...But this way!

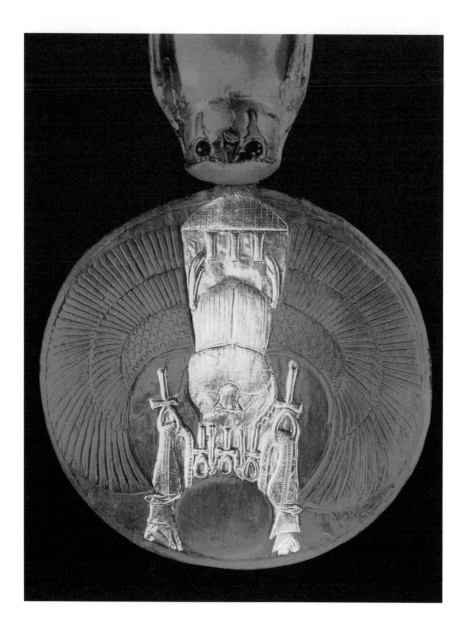

Can you see the spaceship?

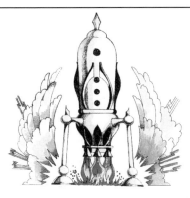

Was God A Star-Traveler?

A passage from the Bible which describes the landing of a huge spacecraft. God in the form of The Star-traveler, helps David defeat his enemies. From Psalm 18:

"In my distress I called upon The Lord for help." (...David is in trouble. He communicates with his protector, The Star-traveler, on Mount Sinai.)

"From his temple (the UFO) he heard my voice, and I am saved from my enemies." (...Message received and understood.)

"Then The Earth reeled and rocked; the foundations also of the mountains trembled and quaked because He was angry." (...The powerful engines of the spacecraft cause earthquake-like reverberations throughout the immediate area.)

"Then smoke went up from his nostrils (emissions from the rocket exhausts) and devouring fire from his mouth; glowing coals flamed forth from Him." (...The heat from the engines burns the grasses, shrubs and kindles stones; it becomes so intense as the engines accelerate, that small rocks in the vicinity of the thrusting, blasting rockets begin to ignite.)

"He rode on a cherub, and flew; He came swiftly upon the wings of the wind.

"He smote mine enemies with arrows of lightning." (...Laser rays from the UFO?)

"The Lord also thundered in the heavens and The Most High uttered his voice at the blast of the breath of thy nostrils." (... The craft rumbled, roared and accelerated overhead.)

OLD EVIDENCE OF A "NEW" PHENOMENON

UFOs, serpents and skulls.

That's a combination of research oddities which could have me classified as a genuine white-jacket case sadly in need of a psychiatric overhaul. However, I like to believe that I am just the same as the rest of the population (take that how you will) and that this line of research is not as crazy as it might at first appear.

I have written before about my interest in the serpent as it appears in ancient mythology around the world. Why is this lowly reptile so often represented as a symbol of knowledge, and why is it shown as a feathered or winged serpent? Wings and feathers indicate an ability to fly but are there any snakes capable of flying? And is there anything in their general behavior which would suggest a superior intelligence? I think not. So again, why was the snake symbol chosen?

Having asked the question, I will later supply a very intriguing answer.

The trail of the mythological serpent has led me to research the prehistoric monuments of the British Isles. Stonehenge and the impressive structures of the mound builders. I have been puzzled by the few skulls found in the very ancient mounds, skulls which are noticeably longer than those of the other Neolithic inhabitants. Did they belong to a special ruling class and does the elongated shape denote a superior intelligence? Or an alien humanoid perhaps? I have an interesting speculation on those questions too but for now let me say that the purpose of this research is to seek linking clues to provide evidence for the existence of a world-wide culture or civilization which predated our present civilization period by thousands of years.

Always in this search I am on the lookout for evidence of UFOs and their possible connection with man's advancement from his animal beginnings.

Now what about UFOs. Do they really exist?

Modern Ufology began in 1947, but of course the subject is much more ancient that that…and it is even part of our religion.

When I was a boy and "forced" to go to church I was always intrigued by the phrase "and He ascended into heaven" – which several of the Biblical chappies apparently had a habit of doing. My childish mind's eye provided me with a picture of a white-bearded prophet being propelled upwards like a rocket until he vanished into the clouds, leaving a crowd of slack-jawed observers to witness this event.

It was a mystery …and as far as I was concerned, utter nonsense. Then, later on, when I began to read Ezekiel's Bible contribution from a UFO point of view, I started wondering if perhaps the "ascending into heaven" reports could be factual rather than fantasy.

The Contactee

In the 5th century before the modern era, Ezekiel described a strange machine which landed close to him. He reported how it came like a whirlwind out of the north and how four living creatures came from it – "they had the likeness of a man." He didn't say they were men, only that they resembled men.

Later in his report, Ezekiel states that high up (in the machine) there was the "likeness of a throne" from where a voice spoke telling him that he was to be taken to the rebellious people of Israel to deliver a message.

Then he goes on: "the spirit took me up… and I hear the noise of the wings of the living features and the noise of the wheels and a noise of great rushing." In other words, he was up, up and away, airborne.

Ezekiel was not a willing or enthusiastic contactee. He remarks that he "went in bitterness" but he obviously had little choice in the matter. He was set down in a place called "tel A'bib (Tel Aviv, perhaps?) amongst the Hebrew captives there, where he says," I sat where they sat and remained there astonished among them, seven days."

Now I'm not quite sure who was astonished, Ezekiel or the captives, but it certainly adds a very human touch to his incredible story.

For many, many centuries, Ezekiel's strange experiences (there were others) have puzzled both the lay reader and the scholar alike – no one was able to provide an acceptable explanation of them.

It is only now, in the age of flight and the new age of UFOs and UFO contactees, that the story begins to have relevancy. Only now can we understand what may have happened to Ezekiel and what he attempted to describe.

We have several modern day instances of people being "taken up in spirit" (that is, taken aboard an alien craft in mind-controlled condition where they had no power to resist what was happening to them) and there are a number of accounts of people, contactees, being taken for aerial jaunts.

I think we can believe Mr. E.'s biblical experience, or at least give him the benefit of the doubt. Anyway, I'm going to use this account to establish the point that UFOs DO exist and that they have been around for thousands of years!

SECRETS FROM THE UFONAUTS

In continuing with the subject of UFO contactees, that is, the experiences of people who claim to have been contacted by Ufonauts in close encounters of the third kind:

Patrolman Herbert Schirmer is a contactee who, under hypnosis, was able to produce a detailed account of his meeting with the crew-leader of a UFO in 1967.

I was especially intrigued by his reference to the badge or insignia displayed on the tunic of a Ufonaut – a winged serpent. Man has been using the symbol of the serpent in connection with knowledge and wisdom for thousands of years and it has always puzzled me as to why the ancients chose it. Now we have this incredible story of a meeting with a space Being, a possessor of knowledge which we do not yet have, and he is wearing our serpent symbol.

Could it be that these same extraterrestrials of today were visiting and meeting with our ancestors thousands of years ago? Did our ancestors see the winged serpent insignia and adopt it because it represented the civilizing knowledge which was being given to people all around the globe?

I feel the time is not far off when the answers to these questions will be forthcoming.

Other Contacts

There are many cases on record where humans have allegedly been taken aboard alien spacecrafts, of speaking with occupants and in some cases being taken on a fast and mind-boggling trip. The accounts given by these privileged humans (under induced hypnosis) are remarkably similar, as for instance in descriptions of the alien beings. If you remember, Schirmer described the crew-leader's eyes as being slightly slanted, yet not like those of an Oriental.

Barney and Betty Hill (Interrupted Journey) described their Ufonauts' eyes as extending further around the cheekbones than humans, while George Adamski, who was probably the first contactee of the modern era, described his visitor as having an extremely high forehead while the eyes were large and slightly aslant at the outer corners.

It would seem that they are all describing the same species.

There are similarities also in the information given to the contactees regarding the propulsion or motive force of the space vehicles.

Schirmer, when questioned by Loring Williams under hypnosis, explained that… "The ship is operated through reversible electromagnetism…a crystal-like rotor in the center of the ship is linked to two large columns. The crew-leader said those were the reactors. Reversing magnetic and electrical energy allows them to control matter and overcome the forces of gravity."

An earlier contactee, Dr. Daniel Fry, who allegedly was taken aboard a flying saucer in 1950, was also given an explanation for the high speed acceleration of the space craft.

"The force which accelerates the vehicle is identical in nature to a gravitational field. It acts upon every atom of mass which is within it, including the pilot and passengers."

And George Adamski was informed by his alien visitor that the UFOs were powered by magnetic-controlled force fields.

When Dan Fry asked his contact for a detailed description of the principles on which flying saucers worked, he was told that he would have to be given an entirely new concept of the laws of physics since our current use of the laws provides only 30 percent efficiency, because they are much too complex.

"Your greatest need is to discover the utter simplicity of the basic laws or facts of nature...then you will be able to produce effects which now seem to you impossible."

Dr. Fry was also given a brief lecture on the importance of returning to all the knowledge we have accumulated and following through with it, or..."go back down the limb on which you are trapped, to the point where it joins the main trunk, and then start up again."

When one considers how inefficient the combustion engine is, I can certainly agree that we are out on a limb regarding propulsion systems. Did we nearly have the right answer some years ago but somehow bypassed it?

We know the fuel supply we now use is eventually going to run out, so perhaps our scientists should take the Ufonaut's advice and begin looking back over the inventions and discoveries of the past. Like they say, "It wouldn't hurt."

It hardly seems possible – but the entire millennium is ended. It is retrospective time, my friend, the year-in-review, and all that.

But this has also been a good period for mystery buffs, what with space exploration reaching new heights with magnificent and revealing looks at Jupiter and Saturn. Many questions were answered with this close-up examination of our distant planet, but even more mysteries were discovered for the scientists to start working on.

In 1979 UFOs were still around and in such numbers that it seemed to be a planned effort to let us know "we are not alone." In fact the year began with a UFO story from New Zealand which had film footage to substantiate it, showing huge white spheres of pulsating lights. The episode was soon followed by reports of UFO sightings from every continent together with sightings of humanoids in silver suits (South Africa) and a "third kind" of encounter or abduction in Miami.

The abduction case occurred on Jan. 3, 1979 when Filberto Cardenas, 45, of Miami was reportedly sucked into a huge purple UFO which had hovered over his stalled car. Three friends who witnessed this body snatching were helpless to intervene as the screaming victim and the UFO disappeared from sight. Ninety minutes later, and nine miles away from the original pick-up spot, a shocked and burned Filiberto was discovered crawling on all fours in the middle of a busy highway. He was rushed to hospital but could not remember anything that had happened during the period of his kidnapping.

(Mysteries involving animals.)

Eight animals were found slaughtered at Newquay Zoo in Cornwall, England. All had been beheaded and drained of blood, and UFO experts found the corpses to be radioactive.

In Calgary, Alberta, Canada, police were baffled by the deaths and mutilations of farm animals but were inclined to think it was the work of some satanic cult.

A report read:

"Eight animals have been mysteriously killed since May," in separate areas of southern Alberta. In all cases the animals' sex organs had been removed, sliced off! The RCMP is not only baffled by the motive for the mutilations but also has no clues as to how the animals died. In all cases there has been no sign of a struggle, no tire tracks or footprints and no traces of lethal drugs in the animals' blood."

People are glancing skywards for an answer to these rather sickening events.

There was so much varied UFO activity being reported in the early months of that year that several space experts and UFO authorities felt that '79 was the year the aliens were finally going to make a specific and definite contact with us... but it hasn't happened to date. Well, it gives us something exciting to look forward to.

Discoveries

As the beat went on, 1979 was an exciting year for many scientific disciplines with discoveries being made in outer space, inner space, under the sea and under the sod.

Deep-sea scientists uncovered an oceanic mystery during the summer of '79, when a team using a submersible went down into the depths of the Galapagos Islands. There they found weird and wonderful fish, monster crabs and giant worms, all previously unknown to man.

One huge worm, several feet long, has no mouth and no gut; how it feeds has still to be ascertained.

The amazing discoveries are at a depth of 2 kilometers, where the pressure is more than 250 times of that on the earth's surface...this was thought to be too extreme for any living thing but once again our mysterious world has confounded the scientists.

And speaking of monsters – a paleontologist, James A. Jensen, uncovered a bone from the largest dinosaur ever found. It was so tall

it could have peered over a 5-storey building, said Jensen, who unearthed the 9-foot shoulder blade in Colorado. With this bone he has estimated that the monster could have been 50-60 feet tall, about 75-80 feet long and probably weighed about 80 tons! (Put that in your oven, Mrs. Flintstone.)

Something a little smaller than that creature, but one that is close to home, so to speak, made marks for another paleontologist to find. This was a trail of seven footprints found in the bed of an ancient lake in Kenya and thought to have been made by an early ancestor of man some 1.5 million years ago. Also in Africa, Dr. May Leakey has found in Tanzania footprints which date back 3 million years! The frontiers of time and space are forever being pushed back and hardly any scientist dares to stand up and make definite statements anymore...tomorrow could well produce new evidence and turn today's pet theories into yesterday's news.

WE ARE LIVING IN THE BEGINNING DAYS OF THE COMING TRIBULATION.

By Anthony Carr

A mighty sign in the heavens shall apprise us of the Great One's return. (Star-traveler, Lord of Lords, King of Kings!)

From the sky Gods you will hear and know everything. I predict Eternal God shall tread upon the Earth and on that day all shall be smitten with fear and trembling—even unto the ends of the earth!

Terrible upheavals! The high mountains shall be shaken, the high hills made low (nearly); all that is upon the earth shall perish, and there shall be Judgment on every man (and woman).

Truly the kind and the righteous He shall save and protect. But not the hypocrites!

Soon will come yet another pandemic Cosmic shock to our collective Psyche. This must occur to modify man's violent behavior, to put back in him the fear of God.

The Antichrist rises out of Africa, evil and black as his heart. To the dark place shall shift the turmoil. He tears the world apart. Once, twice, removed from the East. His sojourn hails his new start. (P.S. We will all recognize him as being from the past.)

But first, behold! He cometh with ten thousand times ten thousand of His holy ones (astronauts), to execute Judgment upon all and destroy the ungodly!

Then the angels (extraterrestrial astronauts), the children of heaven, will again lust after the daughters of men and take unto themselves from among them, wives. Then shall He make peace with the Elect, and they shall prosper.

But before Peace, a great destruction shall be wrought upon the earth, and men shall know agony for five months and three days; he shall see the destruction of his children, and all whom he loves, over and over again, but mercy and peace shall he not attain.

Then a great light shall descend from heaven, coming down like a brilliant, many-colored jewel, and the King of Kings shall step forward to save the world, lest all perish! (i.e., Commander-in-Chief of astronauts, head Honcho—etc...). So sparkling will be his raiment that all the inhabitants of the world will not look upon it directly.

Then shall the Great and Glorious One sit upon his earthly throne thereafter. And his raiment more bright than the sun and all the stars shall hold the children of earth in awe, and He shall judge the world....

* * *

"In God's high place above the world and the firmament, I proceeded to where everything was chaotic and horrible: I saw neither heaven alone nor a firmly founded earth but a place terrible and awful! And it was burning with fire. And I asked the angel (astronaut): 'For what sin are they bound and on what account have they been cast in hither?'

"Then said Uriel, the angel of the Lord, unto me: 'Why dost thou ask, and why art thou eager for the truth? These souls have transgressed the commandment of the Lord and are bound here till ten thousand years, the time allotted for their sins, are consummated:

"And from thence, I went to another place, which was more terrible than the former, and I saw a horrible thing: a great fire there which burnt and blazed!

"Then I said: 'How fearful is this place and how terrible to look upon!' Then Uriel answered me, and said: 'Enoch, why hast though such fear and affright?' And I answered, 'Because of this fearful place, and because of the spectacle of the pain!'

"And he said unto me: 'This place is the prison of the (evil) angels, and here they will be imprisoned forever!' (In this terrible and chaotic corner of the Universe—hell! Yet the good angels — "Souls" — shall bask in the soft light of God's Eternal heaven.)

"Then Uriel said unto me: 'Here their spirits shall be set apart (in heaven and hell) till the great day of Judgment, and the punishment and torment of those who curse forever, and the retribution for their sins, and for even the false Christendom" (the false church).

His Judgment cometh soon: The cities, like unto Sodom and Gomorrah, shall be destroyed first, at the outbreak of Armageddon.

"And there, above the earth and the firmament, I came face to face with the King of Heaven, the God of Glory ("Glory" means bright light), and mine eyes saw the secrets of the lightning's, and the lights and the peels of thunder by which the Lord executed his command."

(Probably aboard a UFO, Enoch was bedazzled and bewildered by the maze of flashing colored lights and booming loudspeakers through which orders were barked. Remember: this is a primitive cave dweller, completely ignorant of electricity—or superior energy power—and all of its multi-faceted uses.)

"I alone have seen this vision, the end of all things, and no man shall see as I have seen." (From The Ancient Book of Enoch, with commentary by Anthony Carr)

The Beautiful Story of Christmas

A modern interpretation by Anthony Carr (of course).

I have always believed that the star of Bethlehem was a UFO, which led the three Magi to the Christ child; that Mary was put into a deep sleep by the Archangel/Star-traveler Gabriel and, through some form of extra-terrestrial artificial insemination, impregnated: —Voila! — a superior human being who was and was not of this world, was conceived (the virgin birth); and the angel of the Lord who appeared to the shepherds "watching over their flocks by night" was most certainly an extraterrestrial astronaut!

A theory that his resurrection could have been the result of the cloning of his body's DNA and his "ascension into heaven"—perhaps to the Mother ship and head-Honcho Star-Traveler—a sort of "Beam me up, Scotty!" will be proffered by someone other than me (for a change), a respected member of the scientific community.

Thus we have the beautiful story of Christmas:

"And God (the "good" Star-Traveler) sent the angel Gabriel (one of his astronauts) to the city of Galilee named Nazareth, to a virgin named Mary who was betrothed to a man called Joseph; and the angel appeared to her, and said, 'Hail, O favored one, the Lord is with you! Do not be afraid, Mary, for you have found favor with God.

"And behold, you will conceive in your womb and bear a son, and you shall call his name Jesus. He will be great, and will be called the Son of the Most High; and the Lord God will give to him the throne of his father, David, and of his kingdom there will be no end; and he will reign over the house of Jacob forever.'

"And Mary said to the angel, 'How shall this be, since I have no husband?' And the angel said to her, 'The Holy Spirit will come upon you (advanced technical type of impregnation) and the power of the Most High will overshadow you; therefore, the child to be born will be called Holy, the Son of God.' (Luke 1:26-35)

"And there were shepherds out in the field keeping watch over their flocks by night. (Again) an angel of the Lord appeared to them and the glory (very bright lights) of the Lord shone around them, and they were filled with fear." (*Throughout the Bible, whenever "the glory of the Lord" is mentioned, it always pertains to brightly shining lights which, centuries before the advent of electricity, certainly would seem like a "glorious" miracle, indeed.)

"And the angel said to them, 'Be not afraid; for behold, I bring you good tidings of great joy which shall be to all men; for to you is born this day in the city of David a Savior, who is Christ the Lord. And this will be a sign unto you; you will find a babe wrapped in swaddling clothes and lying in a manger.'

"And suddenly there was with the angel a multitude of the heavenly host (many celestial astronauts with either oxygen tanks or levitating devices on their backs, often depicted in Christian religion paintings as 'wings'), who were frolicking to and fro, praising God and saying, 'Glory to God in the highest, and on Earth, peace and goodwill toward men with whom he is pleased!'... When the angels went away from them into heaven," etc.... (Luke 2:8-15)

And then there were the three wise men who followed the star of Bethlehem, a very brilliantly lit UFO: "And lo, the star which they had seen in the east went before them (that is, led them, 'till it came to rest, or stop) over the place where the child was."

The Old and New Testaments are rife with stories about Star-travelers, e.g., when Moses brought the people of Israel up to Mt. Sinai: "Thus the Lord used to speak to Moses, face to face, as a man speaks to his friend." (Exodus 33:11)

And as well: Psalm 18 is strongly descriptive of a UFO (unidentified flying object): "In my distress I called upon the Lord for help." (...David is in trouble, so he communicates with his protector, the Star-traveler, on Mt. Sinai.) "From his temple (the UFO) he heard my voice, and I am saved from my enemies." (...Message received and understood.)

"Then the earth reeled and rocked; the foundations also of the mountains trembled and quaked because he was angry" (...The powerful engines of a rocket or space craft cause earthquake-like reverberations throughout the immediate area.)

"Then smoke went up from his nostrils (emissions from the rocket exhausts), and devouring fire from his mouth; glowing coals flamed forth from him." (...The heat from the engines burns the grasses, shrubs and kindles stones; it becomes so intense, as the engines accelerate, that small rocks in the vicinity of the thrusting, blasting rockets begin to ignite.)

"He rode on a cherub and flew; He came swiftly upon the wings of the wind."

"He smote mine enemies with arrows of lightning." (...Laser rays from the UFOs?)

"The Lord also thundered in the heavens, and the Most High uttered his voice at the blast of the breath of thy nostrils." (...The craft rumbled, roared and accelerated overhead. It's no wonder David spent so much time singing praises to the Lord, or Star-traveler, he would have been a dead duck without him!)

The lovely story of Easter:

"Now after the Sabbath, toward the dawn of the first day of the week, Mary Magdalene and the other Mary went to the sepulchre. And behold, there was a great earthquake (hovering space craft causing the ground to tremble?); for an angel (astronaut) of the Lord (head Honcho Star-traveler?) descended from heaven and came and rolled back the stone, and sat upon it.

"His appearance was like lighting and his raiment white as snow." (Probably because of his phosphorus-like, or shiny space suit resembling those that the earth astronauts wore during the 1969 moon landing.) [Mathew 8:1-20]

Watch the heavens for the return of the Star-travelers who will intervene in the affairs of Man and halt the violence: "And I saw the holy city (gloriously brilliant UFO), new Jerusalem, *coming down out of the heaven* from God, prepared as a bride adorned for her husband; having the glory of God, its radiance like a most rare jewel, a jasper, clear as crystal.

"And I heard a loud voice from the throne saying, "Behold, the dwelling of God is with men. He will dwell with them, and they shall be his people, and God, Himself (Supreme Star Chief), will be with them;

"He will wipe away every tear from their eyes, and death shall be no more, neither shall there be mourning nor crying nor pain anymore."

Revelation 21:1-4 & 11

Watch! They are coming! And there shall be peace....

THE END – AND THE BEGINNING!

SUPPLEMENTARY

A QUESTION OF FATE
(Is our destiny in the hands of the "Almighty," or in our own?)

The Misfit.

Not unlike a writer's lot, a mystic's existence is a lonely, miserable one because he dwells too much in his mind....

To set the record straight, I am neither a magician nor an illusionist as are Kreskin, Uri Geller, Sigfreid and Roy, Teller and Penn, David Copperfield, John Edwards—et al. They do not deal with things psychic, per se. Their specialties are prestidigitation, legerdemain (sleight-of-hand)—in short, tricks or pseudo magic. What they *do* practice is not to be confused with pure psychism. (Come to think of it, that which some "psychics" sometimes practice shouldn't be confused with pure psychism, either!)

Now it is certain that they do receive the occasional psychic flash, hunch or gut-feeling during their performances, as indeed we all do, which they will enfold into their act; but don't be misled: *pretending* to read tomorrow's headlines in a sealed envelope or count change in someone's pocket (someone else's pocket, not their own) is not the manner in which a true clairvoyant functions. Not to take away anything from these very talented people who are the best in that skill-demanding profession.

Although able to utilize the occasional psychic impression, even these magicians will admit – or perhaps not – that psychism plays very little in their nightly theatrics – as magical, marvelous and wonderful as those fantastic apparitions may appear to be.

Throughout history the truly great mentalists, illusionists and escapologists such as Dunninger, Houdini, Blackstone, Arthur Ford, perhaps even the mythical Merlin, accepted that all mammals – including man – possess a special faculty beyond the familiar five which enables them to divine coming Earthly (terrestrial) Events before their occurrences.

In prehistoric times and indeed in existing primitive and so-called civilized cultures, this "sense" was and still is essential to survival. Without it, existence would be impossible.

Therefore do not delude yourself into thinking we are so very far removed from Neanderthal man or our four-legged mammalian cousins. Like it or not, we still depend upon our basic instincts for survival. Instincts, hunches – gut-feelings – all are One and The Same, the Same and One.

To pierce the veil, tap the source – the Future – ahh!... Who at one time or another has never agonized over raison d'etre – especially after a personal tragedy, as we ponder the rhyme and reason for it all. Probably in our Heart of Hearts we suspect there is no rhyme or reason for it all – at all. It just is!

The ability to prophesy can be likened to a double-edged sword. It cuts both ways. If this dubious gift is a blessing then it is also a curse. It creates ambivalence, like a terrible accident that one witnesses; too horrible to look at, yet too fascinating to turn away from.

Can we perceive the Future?

More specifically, let's ask for a proper definition of the Future. We are, of course, for the moment talking about Events here on Earth. Good old Terra Firma. Not (for the time being) the Future of any other heavenly body anywhere else in the Universe. Not for instance Mars, Jupiter or Pluto, just here, on Earth. Get it?

So, lets see now... here on Earth, yesterday was once tomorrow and today will soon be yesterday. (So far, so good.) Therefore in reality Earth's Future (as distinguished from "out there in space time" Future), as well as everybody's and everything's Future on Earth, is nothing more than a whole lot of Earth todays strung together leading into Eternity. (Or into the Future!)

To the Eye of The Universe, if The Earth spins fast enough all the "todays," "tomorrows" and "Events" flow into one, great, simultaneous Event and Day. Imagine watching the entire 24-hour life cycle of a firefly – and all human life – from a point far out in Space. The span of human life and that of the firefly is no more significant to the Universal Eye than our observation of the cyclic existence of an anthill colony is to us. (Unless you're kinky for ants!) This theory also applies upwardly and outwardly — to every planet, sun, star, solar system, galaxy, Universe and parallel Universe (or Universi) – all can be crushed into a nano second, or less!

This may be closer to the truth than one might imagine. This also marks the starting point in my attempt to explain the working machinations of all facets of the "sixth sense," also referred to as clairvoyance or psychism. If only I can put down on paper the information delivered me from the "Great Beyond" via my Psychic antenna, then perhaps we may better understand this other dimension. But alas, every discovery has its price. Gone will be the magic and the mystery, the titillating eeriness that sends shivers down our spines.

Accepting theoretical psychism is one thing, proving it factually, how it works and why it works, is like trying to nail jelly to the wall. In short, attempting to demonstrate this "extra" sense is the bugaboo. It's akin to trying to prove the existence of God (whether It, He or She be a Star-traveler or the Universal God that is Nature, or a bit of both).

Testing a "sensitive" or clairvoyant in a controlled atmosphere (laboratory) is often attempted but usually proves unreliable due to the subject's suddenly finding himself in a stress-creating situation. That is to say, a sterile setting with a group of academics at best, or worse, several anti-psychics who wouldn't admit to an accurate clairvoyant prediction if they tripped over one. Most of these scoffers are too pathologically religious or simply just too afraid of the truth to ever want to "stretch" to "see," to "hear," beyond their physical parameters – beyond the finite! I respect an honest skeptic but loath a bigot. Worse, a jealous bigot. His denial is usually attributable to an emotionally vested interest, as our belief system about the Psychic Universe is to us.

This kind of clinical or "Tribunal at Nuremburg" adjudication can be unnerving. Psychic Energy is fickle at best. Several theories about clairvoyance and its workings have been proffered, usually by idiots. Although most are write-offs, being too convoluted or too simple: (— "It's a gift from God!"—) to actually make any sense, the occasional hypothesis is quite brilliant. Intriguing, even.

People who take a passing interest in the subject have deemed the sixth sense as something Ethereal, Spiritual, Godly and therefore beyond our comprehension. Nonsense!

Psychism or precognition is as much an integral part of our senses as the other five; as tangible (or intangible) and about as easy to explain as the mechanics of thought, sight, smell, touch and taste. The key to understanding Psychism lies in the study of the laws of physics; it is merely another physics conundrum.

We know more or less which part of the brain controls the five senses and even how they work. This we accept without question. However we are at a loss to explain why it works and what exactly it is that animates not only the senses, but life, all life — everywhere!

The part of the brain that purportedly controls the psyche is the pineal gland. Even though the medical profession still has not determined that particular gland's exact biological function, they generally agree that perhaps this one facet of the organ may be true....

The unabridged Merriam Webster Dictionary defines this cranial organ as thus: "...of, relating to, or being a small usually conical appendage of the brain of all vertebrates with a cranium, that is variously postulated to be a vestigial third eye, an endocrine organ, or 'the seat of the Soul.'"

I agree with this interpretation but only in part, because it is my contention (and always has been) that the *entire* neurological or Electrical system comes into play – especially in the moments leading up to our physical death – and interacts with the Cosmos, which is the source of all animate and inanimate life, not only here, but *throughout* all Creation in the Universe. Do they not use Electricity to kick-start inert hearts? And electrocardiograms and electroencephalograms to record Electrical activity of the heart and brain?

To choose or not to choose – that is the question.

Presently two schools of thought exist concerning *time, space, distance* and clairvoyance or, in other words, previews of coming Earthly Events. But remember: we are talking about Future Events *only here on Earth!* Nowhere else in the Universe or Universi because there is another facet of "time" to be discussed later. When referring to the Future (Earth Future) we usually think – if we think about it all –

only in terms of this here planet of ours called Earth. But henceforth when you think of the word "Future" please allow your mind to wander beyond these earthly parameters to include the Great, Yawning Universe in which this speck of dust called Earth precariously sits.

So now let us examine the first school of thought: **That everything already exists. Tomorrow's adventures are as fixed and immutable as aging and dying. There is no such thing as free will or self motivation or even blinding inspiration that comes to us *separately* from the Electrical Cosmos, or so implies the first school of thought.** (Sometimes alluded to as Determinism, Fate, etc.).

An inspiration, like a lightning bolt, flashes through our entire neurological or Electrical system, *which can be likened to a storage battery, but does not originate in us!* It exists exogenously *(outside* the organism*)* but is the synapses (Electrical activity from one brain cell to another) that is simultaneously suffused throughout our Electrical pathways and triggers neurons which in turn allow the receptors in the brain to "receive" an occasional flash of genius. Yet we ignorantly – and arrogantly – continue to take credit for ideas that "strike us out of the blue," as though *we* ourselves *willed* these brainstorms. At the death of the corporeal brain and body, I assert that the Energy which serviced them continues on, containing in that small Divine spark every single image, sound and all knowledge we have ever gained in a lifetime, like a computer chip, which may explain the phenomenon of child prodigies, for those who may embrace reincarnation. (Think memory banks – visually and audibly – of your computer.)

If indeed it were true that we as humans could generate our own Life-Force and ideas endogenously, meaning from *within* the organism, why then can we not create an original idea whenever one is desperately needed. (Such as right now, at this very moment, when I desperately need one to finish this essay?) If we are so terrific – as we seem to believe – and are in complete control of our Destinies, why then do we not have absolutely everything in life that we want – whenever we want it... pray tell?

This first school of thought may suggest that Man is an Electrical creature, a receiver / transmitter of Universal proportions, whose Energy is uninhibited by temporal and spatial bounds and therefore sub-

ject to the vagaries of Destiny, Cosmos, Fate, Electricity – whatever.
It may further suggest that we are not even allowed the choice of
which toothpaste to use or when to shower or bathe; *everything has
been Predetermined*. If this sounds ridiculous, then consider the driver
of a car at the proverbial fork in the road: He decides – or at least he
thinks he decides – to turn left instead of right and gets flattened by
a truck.

The "choice" of direction was as simple – or as ridiculous – as putting on your left shoe first, or vice versa. At any rate, so goes the first
theory: that everything that already exists was Predetermined. There
is no such thing as free will....

It is of course, an agnostic argument, one difficult to prove today,
but "tomorrow—?" (Incidently, I like this theory).

I have yet to hold in my mind's eye an image that has not come
to pass in every eerie detail. In short, the first theory states that the
Future is not a possibility but a reality which already exists, even as
Events on this Earth – including Earth itself – are waiting to be interminably maneuvered into position by the Universal Cosmological
Time Clock (not Earth's time clock), so that these Events can be
played out as they were meant to be. To fulfill their Destiny in Cosmic Time. This *is* Destiny.

The second hypothesis provides a conditional Future that is dependent on what occurs or on what one does "today." In other words,
the Future does not really exist yet; it is there, an amorphous thing,
waiting for us to shape it. This theory, of course, postulates the existence of absolute free will.

"I will do with my life exactly as I choose," a young psychology
student – a behaviorist – once told me. "Good luck," I replied, tongue-
in-cheek. Many years later he admitted to me the error of his ways.
He learned life's lessons, as we all must, the hard way. Experience...
always the best teacher.

No one can change Destiny, the human personality nor the Psyche and for certain no one can change the Universal mind. These are
One and the Same. Unless that same Universal Mind (probably unconscious even of itself) orchestrates the change, everything remains
constant. Nature, incidentally, is merely another term for the Univer-

sal Mind – that great unconscious Universal Power that recognizes – not us, not even Itself, but is God – albeit an indifferent one. This entity is not to be confused with the various Star-travelers who probably visited us over the eons and whom (depending upon which culture you belong to), we have come to worship as God, Allah, Jehovah, etc. For they, too, dwell within the great Cosmic Sphere which is God.

The strange tale told by CBC producer Dale Barnes.

There are many examples bearing out the first hypothesis, that the Future (at least Earth's Future) is indeed fixed. One such story that springs to mind involves CBC producer Dale Barnes, who related this strange tale to Allen Spraggett, famed parapsychologist, columnist (The Unexplained!) and author of 20 books on the paranormal, including *Arthur Ford: the man who talked with the dead!* and *Ross Peterson: The Second Edgar Cayce.*

"A friend," began Barnes, "a fellow CBC producer, was on assignment in Tokyo. When he was through, a direct flight to Vancouver was to deliver him home. Although he was late arriving at the airport he was in time to see his plane taxi along the runway. It lifted off, quickly gained altitude, slowly banked to the left....

"Suddenly it seemed to suspend – just for a moment—in midair, gave a slight shudder, then plummeted – like a rock – straight down and exploded on impact! Everyone died instantly.

"To say he was shocked would be putting it mildly. But wait! – There's more!... Still disbelieving his eyes, he made for the nearest phone – mumbling something about thanking his lucky stars.

"He immediately called his wife to allay her fears about any news bulletins she might have heard about the crash; that he had been late, had missed it, and how it, Fate, must have intervened to spare him – and so not to worry because he would be home on the next flight....

"A few hours later, he boarded the very next aircraft bound for Vancouver. It lifted off, quickly gained altitude, slowly started banking left.... Unbelievably — it, too, went into a stall – a tailspin – and crashed in a fiery ball at exactly the same spot as the first plane! –

again killing not only all on board – but nearly all the people on the ground who were still working to clear the previous wreck's debris!

"My friend was killed along with everybody else.".... True story!... Fate? Did he choose his own bizarre ending? Or had his Fate already been written in the stars and in the sands of time, thousands of years before he was even born?

The sad and eerie dream of Abraham Lincoln.

What follows is an even more bizarre tale, about a beloved American historical figure, the16th President of the United States and his frightening dream about which he related to his wife the following morning. Read on:

...In his exhausted condition Lincoln still wasn't sleeping well, troubled lately by strange and ghostly dreams. One night, in the second week of April, with Mary (his wife) present, his friend Lamon, his secretary Kennedy, and one or two others in the White House, Lincoln started talking about dreams, and Mary commented on how "dreadful solemn" he seemed.

"...I had one the other night, which has haunted me ever since," Lincoln said.

"You frighten me!" Mary exclaimed. "What is the matter?"

"Maybe I'd done wrong in even mentioning the dream," Lincoln said, "but somehow the thing has got possession of me."

"What had possession of you?" Mary asked. "What had he dreamed?" she asked, turning in the general direction of Mr. Kennedy.

Lincoln hesitated, then began in a voice sad and serious: "About ten days ago I retired very late. I had been up waiting for important dispatches from the front. I could not have been long in bed when I fell into a slumber, for I was weary. I soon began to dream...

"There seemed to be a death-like stillness about me. Then I heard subdued sobs, as if a number of people were weeping. I thought I left my bed and wandered downstairs.

"There the silence was broken by the same pitiful sobbing, but the mourners were invisible. I went from room to room; no living person was in sight, but the same mournful sounds of distress met me as I passed along. It was light in all the rooms; every object was familiar to me; but where were all the people who were grieving as if their hearts would break? I was puzzled and alarmed. What could be the meaning of all this?

"Determined to find the cause of a state of things so mysterious and shocking, I kept on until I arrived at the East Room, which I entered. There, I met with a sickening surprise. Before me was a catafalque, on which rested a corpse wrapped in funeral vestments. Around it were stationed soldiers who were acting as guards; and there was a throng of people gazing mournfully upon the corpse, whose face was covered, while others wept pitifully.

"Who is dead in the White House? I demanded of one of the soldiers. 'The President,' was his answer; 'he was killed by an assassin!' Then came a loud burst of grief from the room."

As he recounted the dream, Lamon observed Lincoln was *grave, gloomy,* and at times visibly *pale.*

"Well," Lincoln said, "it is only a dream, Mary. Let us say no more about it and try to forget it."...On Wednesday, April 19th, 1865, Lincoln lay in the East Room of the White House, his coffin resting on a flower-covered catafalque, his temple of death. His head lay on a white pillow, a faint smile frozen on his lips, his face pale and distorted in death. The room was hushed and dim, the adjoining rooms festooned in black crepe.

Upstairs, Mary lay in her own room, almost deranged from grief and hysterical weeping, unable to attend the services below.

Suddenly, Mary recalled Lincoln's dream of mournful voices and a dead body in the White House. She cried out miserably: **"His dream was prophetic!"**

(Excerpted from *With Malice Toward None,* by Stephen B. Oats).

Self-fulfilling prophecy of the second hypothesis? Did he, too, shape his own Destiny by going to the theatre? If this were the case, one could argue that he might have altered his tragic Fate by changing the course of events of that terrible day. But if he had, who is to say the alternative might not have been his ultimate destiny, as well? ("...Aside from that, Mrs. Lincoln, what did you think of the play?")

Again, an agnostic argument. But once more I aver that if an individual could possibly manipulate his life's path, he conceivably should be able to manipulate his environment – including the Universe, because in effect this is what the proponents of free will are stating.

Sheer nonsense. The Power controls us, no doubt. We control nothing. Bearing this in mind, it makes sense that Lincoln's prophetic nightmare of foreboding simply had to come to pass in every eerie detail. In my not so humble opinion we cannot escape our Destinies, our "Appointment In Sumara." My Glaswegian granny, who missed her third-class berth aboard the ill-fated Titanic after she arrived in South Hampton four hours late, told me years later, as she lay dying....

"Our Fate is sealed, written in the stars in Heaven and in the sands of Time, laddie, long before we get here and long after we are gone. And when we are gone the Spark, Which is the Electrical Soul, can be likened to a shimmering Teardrop slipping *into* a shining sea, slowly drifting irresistibly toward that vast Ocean of Eternal Being and Nothingness, to merge as One until the Wheel of Life once again turns round to bring us back again and again, forever and ever, unto Eternity."

Thus I believe in the first hypothesis, not the second, and until something or someone convinces me otherwise, I always Will.

Our Unconscious Minds and the Omnipotent Universe are One and the Same Mind that simultaneously interacts and plays games with Each other, which is to say – with Itself. It has dominion over everything – animal, mineral and vegetable – in short, it has dominion over Itself. (Or conversely, maybe not even over Itself!) It *is* the Master Puppeteer of all our actions, whether we like it or not, or believe it or not.

One single Electrical particle of this Power, which we refer to as our "individual mind," not withstanding sleep or wakefulness, can occasionally wander back and forth across Earth's past, present and Future *if* the Electrical frequencies are harmonious and because it is part and parcel of the Electrical Whole. Yet *beyond this planet's sphere of influence there is "no time"* as we understand the meaning of the word: only that mighty cauldron and convention of all Times! The Great Uncreate Primordial Sea of Eternal Being.

I'm convinced this "Receptacle of Times" contains an audio-visual record of every act and every event ever committed or experienced by man – including the images and sounds of good old Earth herself, harkening back to the beginning of Time. Why even the Fate of the Universe is Itself probably recorded within It, like photographic images created by a Super Cosmological Camera. Perhaps that is what is meant by the biblical reference to the eventual opening of the "Book of Life," a Cosmic computer-microchip, video and /or audio-cassette, DVD (digital video disc) of everything each of us has ever done. (Heaven forbid! — Literally!!)

I can only wonder whether Future (Earthly) Events actually do *"physically"* exist out there, or merely their shadows, the photographs, as it were, like movies in storage waiting to be retrieved from the Past, Present and Future!

(Incidentally this is a good argument for alleged sightings of ghostly apparitions, especially as they appear dressed in period costumes; after all, if ghosts truly exist they certainly wouldn't be wearing garments but would – or should – appear as no more than a hazy mist).

Personally, my *feelings* are in accord with the "shadows and photography" theory. Therefore a psychic, a much more "sensitive" Electrical creature, tunes his or her antenna into this plurality of "all times" and retrieves from these "stored" Cosmic Videos, images and information pertinent to his client. (The "holographic images" theory).

We are Electrical creatures, part and parcel of the Electromagnetic *Spectrum* which permeates and Is the unfathomable Universe animating all life. The more Electrical – or highly strung – the individual, the more psychic he or she is and better able to lock into the Universal Electromagnetic Spectrum.

And naturally, the more Energy pulsating through the "sensitive Psychic," then the quicker will his corporeal body break down, particularly if it isn't very robust to begin with, like an overloaded storage battery resulting – sooner or later – in physical, emotional and psychological attrition.

Laugh clown, laugh.

First the body breaks down, then the Nervous Energy, no longer capable of being contained by its banks, overflows and goes wild, resulting in illness or bizarre behavior. Most true mediums are usually ordinary, charming, child-like and even immature folk (myself included); consequently, they naively view this harsh old world through rose-colored glasses and for the most part are warm and trusting – in the beginning – until life takes a couple of good swipes at them.

Psychics have a tendency to shun society as they grow older. Slowly, insidiously, a deep mistrust of people begins to develop, bordering on misanthropy, a result of years of derision and frustration. But life goes on. So they develop and foster a Pagliaci complex of "Laugh clown, laugh...."

> *As the years roll by and the rose-tint wears thin,*
> *From Life's realities he takes on the chin;*
> *And sometimes playing both husband and wife,*
> *He ministers their needs be he great or a mite,*
> *And listens to stories both day and all night;*
> *No wonder these souls, from all of the strife,*
> *Eventually burn out ... for such is their plight!*
>
> (With apologies to poets everywhere).

Not only are they trying to sort out everyone else's problems – but their own, as well! These individuals possess great inner strength, but lack the physical constitution of the Philistines to do battle with the world for very long.

In the end they become frustrated, hurt, bitter, resentful and then, finally, quietly withdraw from the world into a hermit's existence, wrapping their dark cloak of contemplation tightly around them.

Generally speaking, Psychics have very labile nervous systems that cannot tolerate much stress, hence the alternative appellation for a medium is *"sensitive."* For this reason they are prone to more illnesses than normal – mostly nervous disorders, stroke and the like. One cannot continually and continuously exude Electromagnetic Energy without blowing a fuse.

So-called hypochondriacs, *whose general ills may not always be imaginary*, undoubtedly possess repressed Psychic Energy – something analogous to a capped volcano. This leads to another problem – booze and drugs.

Psychics should never drink. No sir-ee! Yet it is these same ultra-sensitive people who incline toward excessive use of liquor and drugs because psychics, mystics and the like, tend to be sicklier and more neurotic than most people because of their sensitive neurological systems: pills, hard liquor and drugs become the illusory escape route from their fears, hobgoblins and ghosts.

Because "sitters" and "readers" (more appellations) depend on this elusive flow of Psychic or Electrical Energy – which cannot always be relied upon – for their livelihoods, they are besieged by even more anxieties piled atop an already overloaded circuit board, compounding their neuroses.

Clairvoyants do not have a union. This oft-times can be quite disconcerting. Since, as I have already stated, the Psychic Energy is not always there every time he does a reading – whether tete-a-tete, over the phone or on television or radio – he is always on tenterhooks, not knowing what, if anything, is going to be revealed to him by his Third Eye.

Occasionally clairvoyants lose their powers for no apparent reason. It may last for days, weeks, even years. Then either they lose their confidence – or worse, their credibility, as sometimes happens – and begin to resort to nefarious means to make ends meet.

Eventually anxiety and guilt (if they possess any conscience at all) will set in because they *are* true to themselves, in a positive way, which means they earnestly wish to help others; as opposed to those who are true to themselves in a negative way, which means they care not one jot what they say or do to their clients, acquiring money being their only motivation. And the latter will include, of course, the shoddy, storefront fortune-telling joints with which we are all familiar: the "Madame Lavenia"-type of reader who tells unfortunate, lonely souls that they are under a curse and that it will cost them mucho dollars – (usually everything they've got)– to have it removed.

There is no such thing as a curse. "Que sera, sera" ("What will be, will be") *is determined* by the Universe. Incidently, *no human being can curse another* unless that being lets himself believe it. Good or bad luck is merely a case of the placement of the planets in The Cosmos at the time of birth. These people are *despicable*, and I call them not fortune-tellers but "un-fortunate" tellers! By the way, the secret to cursing someone is patience; if you wait around long enough bad things happen to *everybody*, at some time or other in their lives. The trick is to be right there, on the spot, when it happens so you can say – "Nyaaa-nya-nya-nyaa-nyaaaaa – I told ya so!"

Of course the ideal situation for a medium is one who does not need to take money for his abilities and therefore will not feel obligated to perform on the spot, like a trained seal. In other words, it would help to be independently wealthy.

However life is far from ideal.... There are no monies provided to support retired psychics as there are for ex-boxers, actors, etc., and so they don't always operate under the most favorable conditions. It is no wonder that they are always fearful and neurotic.

When the world has passed through this current period of philistine greed, we will then train our future psychics and oracles in the same rigorous manner that we now discipline our crack military and athletic teams (minus steroids) and place them in positions of respect that they once enjoyed, similar to the Delphic Oracle in ancient Greece. (Are there steroids for psychics?) I sincerely believe all psychic readers should be examined and licenced by a review board, just as are police, physicians and taxi drivers.

Every civilization has had its seers and mystics whose abilities were highly regarded and revered. A new day is dawning, and soon an ancient respect for the arcane sciences will once again prevail. Remember: **psychic phenomena is merely the ability to comprehend the laws of physics**, in this case laws pertaining to human and Cosmic Electrical Energy, Life Force, Soul – or whatever you choose to call the Power that animates all and everything.

How do the interrelated parapsychological properties operate? Remember I suggested that man is an "Electrical" being, as are all living creatures, and as such he is subject to the unpredictable behavior of Electrical Energy – Energy that sends and receives pulsating signals (or telepathic messages) like a radio or television station? This Electrical Power, the Unconscious Mind, is suffused throughout all Creation and Is That Which some have come to regard as the Universe, Universes (Universi) – or the Living Mind of God.

Thought, Consciousness and Unconsciousness *is* our one and *only* source of Power, the Piper to Whose tune we all and everything must dance (and pay). Therein lies the answer to the question of transmitting and receiving telepathic or intuitive Energy.

* * *

I wish to pause at this point and remind you that we are now *not* talking about "Future" predictions *here on Earth*, which we discussed earlier, remember? If we were, they would then be called clairvoyant visions of "Future *Earthly* Events," and *only* on Earth. What we are now talking about is telepathy, which is *instantaneous "present"* thought or image transference – immediately! – from one person to another the moment it occurs, as a child's distress is immediately "felt" by its mother whether the mother be across the room, across the World – or the other side of the Cosmos!

Telepathic vibration is no more (or less) than Universally pervasive Electricity– throughout all, as is musical vibration – literally! To wit: The *Toronto Star* recently reported (2003) a story from a world famous observatory that said it recently discovered a supernova, some trillions and trillions of light-years away (through the Hubble telescope) that emitted a vibratory musical note that is fifty seven octaves below middle C on the piano. So there!

At this point we should give some thought to "Light Speed," and beyond; which is to ask how fast Electrical Power, Energy or Thought actually travels (without our having to get into questions concerning the mathematics of astrophysics, about which I know absolutely nothing), and concentrating only on the philosophy of it all. I shall painstakingly, inch by inch, in layman terms (the only terms I know), try to explain how this is not only possible, but quite probable.

Consciousness, Unconsciousness, Thought, Instinct, Universal Power, Energy, or God (pick one, none, or all of the above) *are One*

and the Same, in my opinion. But also, and this too must be clearly understood, the Universal God should not be confused with the God or
Gods of the Bible (which includes the five Mosaic books also known
as The Pentateuch), the Koran and Hindu's Upanishad / Vedic scrip-
tures who, in my opinion, were Star-travelers! But that's another story.
(...Yeah, I know—get out the net, he's goosin' butterflies again!)

But when a *thought* or a *feeling* – that piece of *the all pervasive Universal Electrical Power* – is transmitted through the Ether, then that
Spark may travel at least as fast as the speed of light (186,000 miles
per second), but in all probability – much faster! This is, of course,
based merely on our finite human *Earth* time calculations, these
"words," "terms and expressions" which in reality are only "grunts" and
"noises" we use in a futile attempt to explain things to each other we
barely understand.

Yet if this be true, that thoughts and feelings travel at such incredible speeds, then it explains *The Enigma of Intuition or Telepathy* –
again, which is not about Future Events on Earth but about instantaneous "words" /"thoughts" / "feelings"– or put another way – about
Electrical transference between two or more people in the same
room, at opposite ends of the globe or even greater distances such as
far-off planets, galaxies and plural Universes! And with this last pro-
nouncement, we are now ready to begin talking about clairvoyance
and telepathy in relation to different Time Zones, *not only on Earth*
(although that too), but on other planets in other parts of the Cosmos,
as well.

For example: If I "think," "feel" or "see" (in my Mind's Eye) that
something is wrong with my mother or father, sister, brother, husband, wife, son, daughter, dog, cat, etc. – at the exact moment that
they are experiencing it too, then this is telepathy – which means understanding the "message" the exact moment it occurs no matter
where it occurs, anywhere in the world or the Universe, and is *not* to
be confused with "clairvoyant flashes," premonitions – or what we
refer to as "Future" (here on Earth) Events; and for that matter, should
not even be mistaken for retrocognitive readings (something I forgot
to mention earlier), which means "images and sounds" of people and
events, *here on Earth*, which are "heard" and "seen" from the (Earth's)

past and are often mistakenly interpreted as though occurring in the "present" or even "the Future" of *our* lives – instead of being "past" (Earth) Events and pictures and *shadows* of people who *have lived, died and gone on ahead.* Images still very much prevalent and present in *this* realm and sometimes *misinterpreted* as ghosts!

The above theory concerning the three Earth "senses" of time (Past, Present and Future), and World Events we sometimes "pick up," is inextricably woven throughout the "sixth sense" fabric of All Time(s), and begs another question which entails yet another theory... that along with light-speed there is something which suggests that Thought / Energy can and *does* travel at a speed much-much faster than light-speed!

This deals with the now familiar theory of tachyons, or quantum waves or particles, and means, literally, "things that go very fast" – so fast, in fact, that they move *faster* than light-speed itself and can go backwards and forewords in Time, like a movie in reverse. To be-labor a point I tried to make earlier: As in a film, only the "images," not the actual "physical" properties, such as corporeal people, can travel back and forth. Because an actual "physical" person or a property, zapping between or through the "Fabric of Space," would then be in the *present* of that particular world –- Mars, Jupiter, Uranus, etc. – whether that planet *currently* be in the dinosaur or Nineteenth Century period. In short, only the "images and sounds" recorded in the Electrical Heavens, whether they be living or long dead, can travel through the Great Time Continuum, because they *are* only "sounds and pictures," but living or solid bodies or properties cannot.

Whether we are debating the Light Speed or Tachyon theory, I think "It" – in one way or another – explains the workings of intuition and telepathy. (Instantaneous thought / image projection or travel, reminiscent of the old "Flash Gordon" molecular transporter: "Now you see him, now you don't, now you do.")

Hopefully you now have a foggy grasp (a fogginess to match my own) of how *mental* images and messages can – like photographs or words faxed or broadcast overseas – cover vast distances in less time than it takes to blink an eye. Simple isn't it? All this transcends spatial, temporal and physical limits, rendering distance and (Earth) time meaningless. We may *now* cogitate on the workings of mental telepathy and clairvoyance, not only on planet Earth but everywhere in the galaxies (*including* Earth), and even physical teleportation ("Beam me up Scotty"), but always in the "Present time" of that particular planet, in whatever galaxy.

I predict in the not too distant (Earth) Future that physical properties (people or any other solid objects) will be teleported – not only to remote parts of *this* globe – but to other celestial bodies – yet they will always be in "the present," relatively speaking, of that particular world in the same fashion that our creators, the Time or Star-travelers, teleported themselves here thousands of years ago, but in the "then present "of *this* world.

In like fashion, I have limited my analysis of Psychic Energy specifically to "intuition" or "telepathy" (which is instant thought, image projection, or travel) to the "present," meaning the *present* of this world, I have limited it to that "gut reaction" which lets us know when something is going to happen – good or bad – to someone you care about (or don't), in the same room, down the hall or across the ocean.

The other part of the Psyche, the part which sees "Future" and "Past" (Earth) Events (and sometimes Events on other planets), may entail the study of the tachyon or wave / particle theory which (and this bears repeating) describes things-that-go-fast! – so fast that they may go backward and forward in Time, or actually dissolve *through* the Fabric of Space Time so quickly that "things" disappear and reappear elsewhere without any passage of time whatsoever, much like "stepping through" the blades of an electric fan spinning at full tilt.

This is called "sympathetic vibration," which means if you were spinning "in sync with the blades of a fan," as an analogy, you would only need step *between* the blades, so to speak, to enter an entirely different dimension – thus, eliminating the necessity of a spaceship traveling across oceans of galaxies and trillions of light-years to get from one place to another. In other words, you simply dissolve from one Galaxy into another instantaneously without any passage of Time whatsoever. I wonder what the "thought" and "Psychic" speed ratio is to the speed of light?

Whatever the proper appellation for our psychic and physical an-
imation, whether pure Energy, "Lightning" (see Mary Shelly's *Frankenstein*) or the Light of your Soul; and whether or not you happen to be
one of those people who "shrug off" these things as "mere coinci-
dence" or chalk it up to "too vivid an imagination;" or whether you are
a practising mystic or merely a dilettante, you are in fact both **Telepathic** (instant thought transference here on the Earth or anywhere
in the galaxy) and also **Clairvoyant** (able to make Future, *only on
Earth*, predictions). Your Energy (whatever it is) travels at light-speed
in order to render a Present, Past or Future vision. Believe it! And it
may travel even faster (tachyon or quantum wave theory); however
the resulting "mental" or "audible recording" will always appear or be
heard in the *present of whatever world* – be it Earth, where we naturally refer to it as a "Future Event," or in the *"present"* time of *any other
celestial civilization in the Universe – or Universes.*

Perhaps the psyche slips through theoretical "Black holes" (im-
ploding rather than exploding stars) that create a gravitational force
so powerful that nothing – not even light – escapes, and then blasts it
(the psyche) out through theoretical "White Holes" (which I imagine
work contrary to Black ones) with the explosive force of a trillion H-
Bombs into various dimensions, simultaneously creating "Future"
(Earth) Events and "present" Events of all *the other* celestial worlds *in
this* Universe and in all the parallel Universi!

The whole of Creation and un-Creation – and whether or not our
own Universe is expanding or contracting – doesn't mean a damn
thing in the big picture. We, It – and the whole mix-mash – simply
may be rushing toward a monstrous black hole to eventually exit
through a comparable white one, thus continuing the cycle of existence, ad infinitum. The Alpha and Omega. Ergo, we are all immortal in this "One Sense."

The Divine Spark in each of us *is Immortal* and at the point of
death leaves the inert body to return to the Cosmos retaining, I am
reasonably certain, not really a human memory, per se, but a micro-
chip or video-like recorded dim perception of Events, sounds and
voices "housed" in the collective Unconscious Universal library, a kind
of vague "sense" of belonging to a vast Ocean of Energy.

This *is* the Power in *each of us* that wanders the Universe and retrieves our nightly dreams (the actual photographs) from the Great Beyond and stores them in our own mini-Electrical computer, the "Individual" Mind, forever; for It is at once and for all Time part and parcel of The Great Universal Library, in the same manner that one bank branch is connected to another by a computer (and our Electrically-run brain is a computer) and can check your credit rating at any other branch in the world simply by inputting your Data. This Power, along with the pictures and sounds contained within us, is you and is what endures after physical death; and I suppose (and perhaps this bears repeating) provides fodder for the reincarnation theory, the Christian Resurrection theory (Star-travelers raising the dead bones and dust which contain a perfect replica of us in our DNA remains), and the Jehovah Witness faith.

It is a memory micro-chip in the form of an Atom, containing a record of everything you have ever said or done. It is there, somewhere in Space, to be retrieved and reinserted into a new player / machine / body – or whatever; this would explain child prodigies (Mozart, etc).

For instance, dredge up in your Mind's Eye an image of a long-forgotten childhood memory of someone you once loved dearly, but who is now deceased. You will notice that you no longer require glasses to "see" and to "hear," in perfect detail and glorious living color, even holographically, the image and comforting voice of your loved one. (This also applies, unfortunately, to negative and unpleasant memories, as well, i.e., war experiences, murder, etc.). Now, hold that picture or image firmly in your Mind. Got it? Now I ask you, what source or power allows you to do that? It's pretty amazing if you take the time to actually think about it. To visualize an experience "in your Mind's Eye" that may have occurred decades ago! I mean, you should really think about that! It's as though you booted up your own private computer which stores absolutely everything you have ever done or said. (And I use "absolutely" in its absolute sense, meaning the Nth degree.) This will remain with you until the day you physically die, after you die and maybe on into the next experience, whatever form and "expression" that experience takes until the "tape" is covered over by another "life experience" with flashbacks, now and then, to fill in the "missing segments "of the previous experience," something perhaps we all call DEJA VU.

Traveling at light-Speed – or faster – a Star-traveler suddenly appearing in our world would always be physically in Earth's "present," but never "physically" in Earth's Past or Future... if you can follow this: "photographs," "images" or "sounds" of Earth's Past or Future – and even of its peoples – yes, photographs – but *never the physical* entity itself, whether "object" or "person."Never!

Even though the "scientific world" is still at the talking stage about celestial wanderings and traveling Psyches (not Psychics), people and other solid objects will be able to travel via the above mentioned "speed-modes," but again the entity will always be "physically" – as I keep emphasizing because of the necessity to drive it home – *in the present of whatever world in the Cosmos he happens to find himself, but never "physically" in the past or Future of that particular world.*

Actual "physical" time traveling by Earthlings within this world or to any *other* celestial body (as compared to "psychic" time-traveling) is impossible at this point. But not the photographic images taken by The Cosmic Camera (electrons, protons, neutrinos, etc.). These pictures of everything and everybody – Past, Present and Future (remember we are now *back* to talking strictly about Earth time here) – already exists somewhere out there in the Great Beyond and now and then can be "psychically" or, even occasionally with the physical eye, visually retrieved (i.e. ghostly appearances; specters of people dressed in period costume, for instance, which are merely "former" Earthly Events and pictures of dead people, historical or common place, captured on Cosmic videotape or movie film, then trapped in the Time Warp of a "never-ending (repetitious) loop," as the television and movie industry refer to it). "A Never-Ending story." Ditto for early television broadcasts of I love Lucy and The Honeymooners. Finely tuned to the proper "Frequency," and using correct "equipment," whether "psychical or technical," it *can* be done. Because those shows are also out there – somewhere!

Even though a Star-traveler visiting Earth could conceivably show us images and photographs of coming (Earth) Events using a "Cosmic

Camera," so to speak – and since we are now postulating the first hypothesis: that all Events on Earth and elsewhere in the Cosmos are Pre-Destined but may occur "here" a split second "after" or "before" they do out there in Creation – yet that same old "solid" or "physical" Star-traveler *himself* will *always* be in the "here and now," in this "present," on Earth, or in the *"present" of some other Celestial place.*

The Bible speaks of "The Book Of Life" wherein all deeds are recorded and "shall be opened on Judgement Day." As a man liveth so are his acts played out here on Earth and in the Celeste, whether he believes he has control over his actions or does not believe. (Do we have control over the music we play? I doubt it, although the jury is still out on this point.) Perhaps these Events are captured in the galactic Book of Life, a Universal storehouse of individual videos. The ancient Book of Enoch states: "Enoch was taken up to Heaven by God and shown seven Heavens and seven worlds, and the Future of *our world...*" or perhaps he was shown only the "movie trailers" of "coming events."

I speak of the Universe's ability to function as a Cosmic Camera, Television or Radio and its power to photograph and record Events, in the way that the electronic media does.

I refer back to the example of sending a photograph through a machine (Fax, for instance) or a television or radio broadcast across the sea, and I believe – no, I "intuit" that *everything* we do in this life is photographed by Nature, which is to say, the Eternal Power, and will be revealed to each and every one of us at some point; either at the very instant of our physical death (as in: "I saw my life flash before me!") or at some other designated Cosmic Time.

This theory of the Universal Camera, I'm certain, applies equally to the study, art and science of astrology. If you do not understand the underlying principle of astrology, it is this: The Cosmic Camera takes a picture of all the planet's positions at the *moment* of your birth (called a natal chart). It is the same analogy as the *I Love Lucy* show; it is that particular photo of the position of your planets "frozen in time and space" that is floating around somewhere out there – forever, and is eternally connected to your Electrical Self until the day you die – and possibly beyond! Then as you continue your journey through this predicament called Life, those same planets – of which a photo was taken at your birth – continue to travel (called transits) through the Heavens to *eventually make contact with that original picture* of themselves, thus triggering new Events during your sojourn in this place called Earth.

Get it? Good. (Now explain it back to me, because I'm more confused than ever!)

The current transiting planets (which means where the planets are in the heavens – *now, today*) make contact with **that Universal photograph of themselves** – the photograph forever attached to you! – and create interminable life adventures for you! Some pleasant, some...not so pleasant! But these create the best learned lessons, for they are the hard learned lessons.

And people who "hear voices" are generally not always crazy, but may be highly intuitive and sensitive, as are people who "see things!" These "voices and pictures" are carried through the Ether to be "picked-up" by "living individuals" (on Earth) whose nervous systems are so finely-tuned as to be able to "tap" into those "recordings" – whether audially or visually – of people who "are now" or "once were!" People who are innately aware of Universal perturbations.

Incidently, this may explain some causes of schizophrenia. Some people – not all – have nervous systems that are so finely tuned, due to an abundance of Serotonin circulating throughout the brain's labyrinthine pathways, which would behave like the fluid in a car battery (old makes of cars), as to act in much the same way a receiver / transmitter does, causing the individual to "pick up" multifarious voices from the Ether – indeed, from all over Creation – voice recordings from entities both living and dead – and beyond this world – that would drive him absolutely mad – literally! It can be likened to a radio with a broken dial – his being bombarded by thousands, perhaps even millions, of voices.

Perhaps psychiatry, instead of whacking him out with drugs, might be better served if it structured a different paradigm, approaching the "disease" by explaining to the patient exactly what is happening to him, thereby allaying what must seem to him an overwhelming fear of the unknown, and then help him control this power for the betterment of all – especially himself!

Some recent notes by Anthony Carr

Recently this author read an article in a scientific journal whose headlines screamed: "**Archaeologists make startling discovery!**" The story alleges that a member of their group took a three thousand year old Etruscan clay pot, placed the relic on a potter's wheel and began spinning it, which is the way the ancients originally made pottery – by placing a lump of clay on a flat wheel and whirling it around with a foot-and-pedal mechanism while they shaped the mass by hand or stylus (a pointed implement, like a record player's needle, which leaves grooves similar to records).

With great care, the scientist gently nudged a pointed stick against the cylindrical indentations in the ancient jug and – behold! – **the ancient vase speaks!** Hear the sounds of antiquity! Strange sounding tongues, the clatter of activity, noises of people – coming and going – haggling in the market place, the thud of animal hooves against soft earth, the braying of donkeys.

As the clay was being shaped by its original creator, his primitive needle-like point against the pot – acting much like today's recording devices – picked up the ambient sounds of its environment, which is what this group of archaeologists were hearing!

Now, if we take this fabulous discovery just one step further – which is, that visual images as well as audio sounds can be picked-up, recorded, then stored in the "Great Recording Studio in the Sky"– well then, there you have it.

The following is from **The Soul of the Universe,** by Dr. Gustaf Stromberg, late astronomer at Mt. Wilson Observatory:

"At death our brain *field*, which during our life determined the structure and functions of our brain and nervous system, *is not destroyed.*

"Like other *living fields,* it contracts and disappears at death, apparently falling back to the level of its Origin. All our memories are indelibly engraved in this field and after our death, when our Mind is no longer blocked by inert matter (our bodies), we can *probably* recall them all, even those which we were never consciously aware of during our organic life...."

Some psychics say they contact this Etheric Great Heavenly Store-house (that the ancient Hindus called The Akashic Records) through clairvoyance or out-of-body experience, and thus they receive information about past history or past lives. American Medium Edgar Cayce often said he used Hindu ideas to look into past lives to find reasons for health, personal and marital problems in the current lives of clients. The process is variously described as "tuning into an astral television or radio broadcast." Some say they encounter spirit guides who assist them in locating information.

...And finally, whatever your beliefs or no (that is, if you believe nothing) – believe this: That your Sensorial Self (which is your Electrical Soul, your True Essence) will forever languish in unimaginable agony at The End of the Cosmos where only Chaos and dark storms rage, if you have committed heinous crimes. (Perhaps an exploding Super-Nova in Space is the equivalent of the Eternal Lake of Fire mentioned in Holy Scripture.) But for the gentle souls, whose innocent blood has been spilt, is reserved the Soft, Quiet Light of Heaven at the opposite end of Eternity. Who knows... maybe "somewhere over the rainbow" does exist after all.... Somewhere. **(Anthony Carr)**

Bibliography:

A history of Anthony Carr's fulfilled
(and "_documented_") prophecies!

HERE ARE SOME OF ANTHONY'S FULFILLED PREDICTIONS FROM 2005 - AND PREVIOUS YEARS

Attack on America by Arabs! "New York will be devastated by Arabs who wear the red turban and whose emblem is the crescent moon and star" (9/11); major advances in spinal cord research: "Dead legs will walk again;" the murder of Pope John Paul I (poisoned!); the death of Princess Grace; the Faulkland Islands War; the tragic downing of the Pan Am Flight over Lockerbie, Scotland; the last (1994) "Killer Quake" in California; the "Chunnel" between England and France; the horrific Mideast overture to Armageddon (Desert Storm); the eruption of Mt. St. Helens; the bombing of the Statue of Liberty and "The White House Dome" (Senate Building); the assassination attempt on Pope John Paul II and former U.S. President George Bush; the near death experience of Bloc Quebecois Leader Lucien Bouchard which claimed his leg; ex Prime Minister Brian Mulroney to become the first former PM in the history of Canada to be accused of corruption and racketeering.

SEVERAL ANTHONY CARR PREDICTIONS FOR 2003— AND BEYOND FULFILLED

San Francisco Bridge—Destroyed!
Statue of Liberty—Destroyed!
"Lady Justice" Superior Court Building—Destroyed!
All destroyed!—but only at the Movies!
(FROM THE CORE, 2003)

And this 2004 prediction: "New York City swamped by a tidal wave! I 'see' flooding in New York! Fires throughout posh Beverly Hills and surrounding area! Destruction of San Francisco Bridge! Statue of Liberty! Lady Justice Superior Court Buildings! In this sense the world will be hit simultaneously by a double whammy!"—but again, at the movies, from THE DAY AFTER TOMORROW—and aren't you glad it's happening only in movies... (so far)? But you might remember that a film is often a precursor to real world events, as well as the depiction of reel world events.

I have developed the unusual ability to not only predict actual world events well in advance of their occurrences, but also coming blockbuster movies and front page newspaper stories; specifically their images and photographs. For instance I saw the funerals of Monaco's Princess Grace (Kelly) and that of Princess Diana in my Mind's Eye before they appeared in newspapers worldwide! I saw E.T., THE EXTRATERRESTRIAL, in my Mind's Eye and thought it was an actual coming world event, but it turned out to be only a movie event. Shortly after, I read the palms of the late, great actor Richard Burton. I warned him to take care:

"I see you and a red-headed woman together in a speedboat about to be dashed against jagged rocks!"...at that, Burton glanced up at his manager and asked, "Did you show him the script?" "Absolutely not," came the reply. I had correctly intuited the proposed movie ending... which they then cautiously changed.

It seems most actors live their lives, that is to say, their preferred lives, on stage and in film; therefore many of the scenes I have described herein regarding their futures will be reflected in the work they do, have done and will do in future roles proposed to them, as opposed to their real terrestrial lives which they, along with the rest of us, have come to know and generally despise.

I have long since arrived at the illogical but probably intuitively correct conclusion that the machinations at work in the Cosmos and in our own Psyches are One and the Same Electrical Impulse (for want of a better word that doesn't smack of anthropomorphism or a "personal relationship with God," or some such stuff) that is utilized in movie making, television broadcasts and also in keeping our hearts beating and synapses synapsing.

My point being that even though I arrived at this conclusion circuitously, the Cosmos does not seem to differentiate between real events ...and "reel" events, which lead me to the oft-put question: "Well then, what is reality?" After all, if what the Source shows us in our Mind's Eye can be from "reel" life or "real" life, then wha-a-a-t, pray tell—is real?

And what about when we dream? Is that the true Electrical Us— which is able to wander back and forth across the Universe throughout Space and Time, unencumbered by our physical bodies? And what if we should die in that moment of sleep? (We should be so lucky!) Would that Divine Spark ("The Soul") simply go on dreaming? Probably.

I once saw in my Mind's Eye a terrible tidal wave sweeping across New York City and a gigantic tornado ? the biggest I have ever seen ? utterly destroy Los Angeles! It seemed so real I was compelled to phone Joe Mullins, at The Globe in Florida, and describe to him my vision. He duly received it (with his perfunctory tongue in cheek attitude), then placed it in his desk drawer of "useless information" and quickly forgot about it. When the movie "THE DAY AFTER TO-MORROW" was released in May 2004, here they were, the two disaster predictions ? exactly as I had seen them in my Mind's Eye. I called Mullins to remind him of the vision, just as he was preparing to release a spread of that movie's stills (photographs from movie) in the Globe—in full color—pictures of the tidal wave and giant tornado destroying New York (Manhattan) and Los Angeles, respectively.

Electrical antennae, by-the-by, are the entire neurological system, including the Pineal gland, which acts as a movie projector and recorder of Current, Past and Future events—at least visually, and cares not whether "said events" are from real life or film life. In short, you should understand that this is the application of the laws pertaining to Psychic function. The subtle Electrical, Atomic and Psychic forces of Nature or, if you prefer, our Souls, are at One and is One with the Universe (though corny as it sounds), not separate.

This is the Eternal Power that simultaneously records (in our psyches) all of our experiences—forever.

Any war veteran will tell you he carries with him—always—the horrible images and sounds of what he experienced in battle, never being able to divest himself of the terrible memories until the day he dies, and perhaps not even then...

Fiction writers such as H.G. Wells and Jules Verne wrote about future events and inventions a hundred years before they became fact ? submarines, planes, helicopters, trips to the moon ? although I'm sure at the time they thought their creations were strictly figments of their imaginations, mere grist for the writer's mill, without any thought that they were actually plucking from the Universe images of Future Events and machines, much in the manner Hollywood writers and movie producers do today.

In fact today, August 29, 2006, even as I am currently desperately writing to finish this manuscript before publication deadline, I recently saw a movie—a comedy—called WITHOUT A PADDLE.

There is a burial scene in which the priest/minister recites the eighteenth (18th) psalm!… In all my years of attending movies (considerable—probably thousands!) and the same number of real (not "reel") funerals, I have never, not ever, heard anyone—on or off screen—invoke such an obscure psalm, except of course by me, in a later section of this book, namely: "Was God a Star Traveler?" by which I refer to the psalm to suggest that possibly "God" was and is a galactic star-hopper. This is yet another example of celluloid synchronicity.

Whatever the Electrical process at work which allows us to "snap photo images" and "hear" in our minds the recorded voices, sounds and music of present daily life and activity on Earth, is the same element used in motion pictures, radio and television. It is the same Power.

All events—on stage and in life—are recorded in the Great Beyond, the Cosmic Camera, the Akashsic records or simply put, the Universe. And speaking of which, here is yet another example of predicting a celluloid event: the 2005 Summer Blockbuster War of the Worlds! — as opposed to a true life event on planet Earth. (Or in this instance—off the planet Earth!) In 1991, here is what I predicted, and which is still to be fulfilled….

"A strange vision: I see countless thousands of men, women and children—all walking across desert or plains country with arid hills in the background, toward a bizarre-looking, russet-colored craft, for want of a better description. It looks like a curling stone without a handle. On each side is a huge, round, silver-like fin or wing. It (the curling stone) stands very high up on a tripod affair, with covered or chrome-like fenders covering the top halves of the feet. Interpretation: Before long, I believe there will be a gathering or culling of a percentage of the Earth's peoples by these superior Beings who are responsible for our existence. One reason may be the perpetuation of the human race after the coming natural and manmade holocaust. During this same period great numbers of UFOs will be sighted, flying in three endless lines: one traveling left, one right and one straight up the middle.

"Another strange vision! In my mind's eye there is a figure who wears a gilded crown, or headpiece. He/She also emerges from one of the strange looking crafts. In his right hand, the figure holds aloft something shinning or glowing, and there are four or five other "figures" standing beside and slightly behind this main figure. Interpretation: more Star-travelers!"...

(World Events: predicted 2001, hours prior to Bush's slim win.)

"It won't be long before president-elect George W. Bush plunges the world into war!" and "The Mid-East will explode like a roman candle, drawing all nations ever closer to WW III ..."

These two chilling prophesies I made in 2001, and now that President Bush has indeed precipitated the overture to Armageddon, we are well on our way towards World War III. The 9-11 terrorists must be weeded out. There is no turning back now!

That said, I predict President George W. Bush will be re-elected then assassinated before being thrown out of office, whichever comes first. Ditto for British Prime Minister Tony Blair. In the end, America, Canada and the rest of the free world will come out of this magnificently. All that is required is a little courage, calm and determination to fight when necessary and the Will to do so, for the good life always comes at a cost—the cost of sometimes putting one's self in harm's way. Persistence and determination alone are Omnipotent and will carry us through the coming tribulation: to victory.

Education will not. Hitler, the tyrant, first destroyed all educators and books. Genius will not... unrewarded genius is almost a proverb—likewise talent. Guts, persistence and calm in the face of danger will solve and always has solved the problems of the world created by despots.

We cannot allow a bully to get the upper hand. We can't! God bless the Canadians, Americans, the British—and all our allies!... I'm old enough to remember what we were capable of—and proved!—during World War II.

We have simply forgotten how to do it—and just how tough we can be when push comes to shove! And if we don't get tough soon we are all going to pay an unparalleled penalty for refusing to see the truth! For burying our heads in the sand! Peace will come, but ultimate peace will not come 'till the Star-travelers return. Then will they establish His throne on Earth!!!

Remember what Benjamin Franklin said during the Revolutionary war (or the War of Independence, depending on what side of the pond you were on)? "We must all hang together or most certainly we shall all hang separately!"

God Bless (or should that be "Star-traveler Bless").

ANTHONY CARR'S MORE RECENTLY FULFILED PREDICTIONS—AND OTHERS WHICH ARE UNFOLDING EVEN AS WE SPEAK:

"Whole face transplants and re-plants become common throughout the medical and cosmetic industries for people who have been seriously disfigured, i.e., faces torn off by machinery or destroyed by fire." (Prophesied June 2005 for 2006 "STARGAZER"), to wit: "MDs hail first face transplant!" (Toronto Star, December 1, 2005)

Black in the red? In my Predictions for 2002, I said, "Former Canadian citizen Conrad Black—now Lord Black of Crossharbour—will rue the day he renounced his citizenship to become a peer of the realm. He'll come scurrying back like the proverbial dog with its tail between its legs, when danger threatens!" ...Now its time to pay the piper, both for his hubris and his greed, especially if indeed the stories are true about theft, graft and not returning money to the people after giving his solemn word to do so. His solemn word!! In my book there is (practically) no greater sin! My father—literally on his death bed, said—and I'll never forget it… "If your word is no good, then you're no good!" (Prophesied June 2002, "STARGAZER"), to wit: "Black indicted on eight counts of (U.S.) fraud. (Toronto Star, November 2005)

Mr. Black will lose everything—money reputation and most valuable of all—trust… because trust, once lost, can never be retrieved. His wife, former Toronto Sun journalist Barbara Amiel, may stay until the end only because she is a Scorpio by sun sign, and Scorpios are generally loyal to their friends—even when everyone else has abandoned them. A Scorpio's motto is, "I'm your friend through thick and thin until you cross me, and then it's not "an eye for an eye and a tooth for a tooth" — but two eyes for an eye and two teeth for a tooth!"

*Although a tremendous earthquake will shake the city of Barrie, in Canada, damage will not be severe; however it will lead to the discovery of multiple fault-lines in the area. *(Prophesied June 2005, for 2006 "STARGAZER")

*Sylvester Stallone must guard his health. Moderation is the key word. He'll need to conserve energy because I see him moving ahead by "leaps and bounds"?literally! New Rambo and Rocky flicks are in his future! *(Prophesied June 2005 for 2006 "STARGAZER"), to wit: "Stallone to shoot parts of Rambo and Rocky VI in Toronto. (Toronto Sun, July 2005)

"During a popular Reality Show—a tragic death occurs!… I believe the death will occur on the new 'Reality Boxing' show hosted by Sylvester 'Rocky' Stallone. (Prophesied June 2004, "STARGAZER"), to wit: "NBC's Contender will fight on after boxer's suicide… Najai Turpin (competitor on The Contender) fatally shot himself in the head…" (February 17, 2005, Toronto Sun)

"Actor Robert Blake will be acquitted of murdering his golddigger wife, Bonny Lee Bakely." (Prophesied June 2003, for 2005 "STARGAZER," and National Examiner September 23/2003), to wit: "Actor Robert Blake Acquitted of His Wife's Murder!" (March 29, 2005, CNN.com)

"Tidal waves (tsunamis) seen only in movies become reality! Monstrous circles of water to engulf populated cities as Earth's polarities shift." (Prophesied June 2004 for 2005 "STARGAZER"), to wit: "Giant tsunamis wipe out nearly entire South Asian coastal communities—including Thailand, Sri Lanka and nine other Asian and East African nations—already over tens of thousands dead, total expected to exceed one hundred thousand!" (December 28, 2005, Toronto Star)

"The Empire State Building explodes from a terrorist bomb! In a futile attempt to demoralize America, Arab terrorists, who wear the red turban and whose emblem is a 'star and crescent moon,' are responsible." Also, "the Pentagon bombed!" (9-11, Prophesied, National Examiner, January 2001)

"This Pope dies before years end or very early in the new one...." (Prophesied June 2004, STARGAZER: Predictions for 2005), to wit: "Pope Dies" (March 2, 2005, Toronto Star) "Michael Jackson will mirror O.J. Simpson—ending his career.... Money depleted, spent on payoffs and lawyers, Michael has danced his last waltz and it will take more than a moon-walk to keep him grounded." (Prophesied June 2004 for "STARGAZER" Predictions), to wit: "Jackson Not Guilty." (June 14, 2005, CNN.com)

"Palestinian leader Yasser Arafat will die mysteriously...." (Prophesied June 2004 for 2005 "STARGAZER"), to wit: "Palestinian leader Yasser Arafat dies of mysterious illness!" (November 10, 2004, CNN.com)

"A giant comet like 'object,' visible even by day, will appear on the horizon, heralding momentous global changes." (Prophesied August 2002 for 2005 "STARGAZER"), to wit: "Space Shuttle Columbia Disaster!... It streaked across the sky like a great meteorite at noontime!" (February 2, 2003, Toronto Star)

"The College of Cardinals will elect a German Pope...." (Prophesied March 2, 2005 to Les Pyette, publisher, National Post), to wit: "Jozef Ratzinger, now a.k.a. Pope Benedict XVI, a German." (April 19, 2005, National Post)

"Osama bin Laden is most certainly not dead and will resurface periodically to verbally threaten the free world before he or his corpse is captured." (Prophesied January 2003 for 2004 "STARGAZER"), to wit: "bin Laden resurfaces with election warning!" (October 30, 2004, Globe & Mail)

"The Mideast will explode like a roman candle in 2001, drawing all nations ever closer to WW III!" (Prophesied January 2001)

"I see raging fires around the White House in Washington D.C.!!" (Prophesied January 2001)

"Wrinkled rocker, Mick Jagger, will finally receive his much coveted knighthood," (Prophesied, Toronto Sun, June 2002), to wit: "Mick Jagger was finally knighted."

"A fatal outbreak of Mad Cow disease will strike Canada and quickly spread across the country and the U.S." (Prophesied August 2002), to wit: "Man dies of variant Creutzfeldt-Jacobs disease (Mad Cow) in Saskatoon, Saskatchewan, Canada—and in Toronto's St. Michael's Hospital, August 2005."

"Princess Margaret will pass on in 2002." (Prophesied, Toronto Sun, February 2002), to wit: "Princess Margaret Dies!"

"There will be "a successful bombing of the Staten Island Ferry! New York City will be rocked by multiple disasters; riots, Earthquakes, chemical spills." (Prophesied January 2001 and August 2003), to wit: "10 die in New York Staten Island Ferry Disaster!" (Toronto Star, October 16, 2003)

"The Mighty Eagle will do battle with the cowardly snake—to victory!!! This I prophesy 100%!!!" (Prophesied January, 2001)

"A terrible and certainly unexpected earthquake will hit New York City!" (Prophesied January, 2001). "There will be a terrible plane crash over New York City; hundreds are killed." (Prophesied January, 2001)

"Watch for a sign in the heavens that will shock the world! Like a bolt of lightning—perhaps in the form of a UFO—it will put the fear of God in us!.... I feel a great revelation for the world, as if the entire population is coming to its collective senses and we realize we have to do something before it's too late. We'll help each other and band together for protection and for the sake of the survival of the human race. Reversal of celestial and terrestrial events and properties will reverse polarities and moralities and return us to old-fashioned values." (9-11, Prophesied, Toronto Sun, January 2001)

Jacqueline Stallone

Astrologer Extraordinaire
Writer / Lecturer

January 2005

As an astrologer and author ("STAR POWER: AN ASTROLOGI-CAL GUIDE TO SUPER SUCCESS!" – PUBLISHER, NEW AMERICAN LIBRARY), and after meeting and talking with virtually every psychic on this continent and in Europe – including the late Jean Dixon –, I'm truly and deeply impressed by the extraordinary gifts of the Toronto psychic-palmist, Anthony Carr.

Anthony is gifted paranormally in a virtually unique way. I say unique because where other psychics, seers, clairvoyants, telepathists – and believe me, I've met them all – *they play it safe* – Tony gets bizarre psychic images that have proved amazingly accurate! His ability to see into the future is eerie. to say the least.

In plain English, Tony sees the future. He really does!!! Many of his predictions are seen on television, heard on radio, and have been recorded in print around the world – long before the events occured!

I think you can get a great item out of Anthony by playing up the angle, "the man who sees the future" *before* the event – not after, as most people do.

I am writing this letter as a favor to Anthony. However, I certainly would not vouch for him if he were not good. I think my record as being honest stands on its own merit, around the world. He is uniquely gifted. He truly sees the future! I have worked with Anthony on numerous shows, world-wide.

Sincerely,

Jacqueline Stallone
Jacqueline Stallone